BACK-TRACKING
IN MEMORY

The Life of CHARLES M. RUSSELL, *Artist*

Dear Charlie Russell Rider,
Hats off to Nancy's stories about
Charlie!
With warmest regards,
Tom Petrie
Brian Dippie

Wedding portrait of Charles M. and Nancy C. Russell (1896),
ELITE PHOTO CO., GREAT FALLS, MT. C.M. RUSSELL MUSEUM, GREAT FALLS, MONTANA,
GIFT OF RALPH AND FERN LINDBERG (996.10.60).

BACK-TRACKING
IN MEMORY

The Life of CHARLES M. RUSSELL, *Artist*

RECOLLECTIONS, REFLECTIONS AND PERSONAL
PERSPECTIVES BY Nancy Cooper Russell

INTRODUCTION, PREFATORY NOTE, EDITS,
COMMENTARY, AFTERWORD AND FINAL THOUGHTS BY
Thomas A. Petrie IN COLLABORATION WITH **Brian W. Dippie**

Frederic G. and Ginger K. Renner Research Series

Published by the C.M. RUSSELL MUSEUM   *Great Falls, Montana*

C.M. RUSSELL MUSEUM®
The Art and Soul of the American West

Frederic G. and Ginger K. Renner Research Series
Published by the C.M. RUSSELL MUSEUM   *Great Falls, Montana*

Front Dust Jacket Cover: Russell the Cowboy Artist, Byron Company (New York, N.Y.).
Museum of the City of New York. 93.1.1.9224
Back Dust Jacket Cover: *Joshing Moon* (1918), Charles M. Russell. Petrie Collection.
Front End Sheet: *The History of the West, I* (detail) (1926), Charles M. Russell.
Rees-Jones Collection, Dallas, Texas.
Back End Sheet: *The History of the West, II* (detail) (1926), Charles M. Russell.
Rees-Jones Collection, Dallas, Texas.
Additional manuscript materials by Nancy C. Russell reproduced courtesy of the
Gilcrease Museum, Tulsa, Oklahoma.
(TU2009.39.4038.1-3)
(TU2009.39.4047.1-6)
(TU2009.39.4048.1-6)
(TU2009.39.4064.1-2)
(TU2009.39.4987.1-2)
(TU2009.39.8031.1-2)
(TU2009.39.8035)

Letter to Charles and Nancy Russell (1922), Charles F. Lummis. Gilcrease Museum,
Tulsa, Oklahoma (TU2009.39.4780).

ISBN: 978-1-59152-288-1

For more information or to order extra copies of this book call Farcountry Press
toll free at (800) 821-3874.

sweetgrass**books**
an imprint of Farcountry Press

Produced by Sweetgrass Books
PO Box 5630, Helena, MT 59604; (800) 821-3874;
www.sweetgrassbooks.com

Book design by Jess LaGreca

Printed in Canada

Thomas A. Petrie

For Jane—at halfway to our 50th,
thanks for much more than persevering through
a quarter century of Russell adventures

Brian W. Dippie

For Donna—and our fifty-five precious years
trotting together in double harness

. . . I have been getting material together ever since Charlie has been gone that will have the heart and the meat in it that is necessary to give the world the picture of the Charlie that I knew. . . . The things I read about him . . . lose all the warmth of him and just make an ordinary romantic figure instead of one of the greatest souls this country has ever known.

Nancy C. Russell to Judge James W. Bollinger,
December 11, 1936

Contents

Introduction
by Thomas A. Petrie

WHEN CHARLIE RUSSELL wrote from Montana to inform his family in St. Louis of his plans to marry Nancy Cooper, he invoked the phrase "Bushwhacked by Cupid" using the analogy of the unsuspected shot by Cupid's arrow to describe his decision to abandon what had been an extended adult bachelorhood. Nancy indicates that Charlie's father, Charles Silas Russell, queried his son whether he was prepared to take on the responsibilities of being a husband in light of his footloose and fancy-free years as a cowboy. As it turned out, Charlie and Nancy would enjoy a most fruitful, loving partnership, albeit periodically punctuated with strong confrontations. Charlie was thirty-two and Nancy was eighteen when they married, but despite this fourteen-year age difference she almost immediately brought a complementary business acumen and genuine enthusiasm to the union that translated into her innate ability to market confidently and price boldly his artistic output.

Nancy Russell's indomitable spirit and shrewd pricing strategies enabled the couple to afford building Bull Head Lodge, their beloved cabin on Lake McDonald, in the tenth year of their marriage. This heralded Charlie's exceptional multi-year burst of creativity in artistic output. Almost two decades later, Nancy's continuing financial focus facilitated the dream of their retirement home in Pasadena, California. Because Charlie died just over a month after their thirtieth wedding anniversary, he did not live to see the completion of "Trails End," as Nancy chose to call it. Nevertheless, the overall results from their union of talents were far beyond those that would have been achieved absent her active involvement.

As Nancy relates in these pages, she challenged Charlie to do his best and he rose to meet those expectations. He once said, "We're pardners . . . she could convince anybody I was the greatest artist in the world. . . . An' y'u jes' can't disappoint a person like that." Many have noted how important Nancy's business and negotiating skills were to the evolution of his talent, including Charlie receiving national as well as international acclaim as Montana's preeminent Western artist during and after his lifetime. Charlie openly and frequently acknowledged this reality and was genuinely proud of Nancy's integral role in shaping his success.

As several of the tales herein demonstrate, it could legitimately be surmised Nancy also learned how to effectively "bushwhack" collectors and enthusiasts who loved the Old West and the history of its people. For example, Nancy's effective cultivation of the wealthy art collectors Malcolm S. Mackay and Philip G. Cole ensured that there would be very fine assemblages of Russell masterpieces that ultimately brought critical mass to important art institutions. These esteemed collections now comprise cornerstone holdings of the Montana Historical Society and the Gilcrease Museum in Tulsa. In turn, those institutions undoubtedly paved the way for the subsequent focus by others on the Russell art legacy, notably including the C.M. Russell, Amon Carter, Sid Richardson, Whitney Western Art Museum at the Buffalo Bill Center of the West, Norton, Stark, and Rockwell Museums. In addition, Nancy's own collection, acquired following her death by C.R. Smith, is now on prominent display at the Jack S. Blanton Museum of Art at the University of Texas at Austin.

Given Charlie's reference to the ambushing term regarding Nancy's capture of his heart and attention, I was initially inclined to title this manuscript with Charlie's phrase "Bushwhacked by Cupid." However, eminent Russell scholar Brian Dippie alerted me that there was evidence in the Britzman archives at the Helmerich Center for American Research at the Gilcrease Museum that Nancy's actual title for her memoir is the one that now appears on the cover.

The approach that Nancy Russell took in her endeavor to write a biography of her famous husband is evocative in certain respects of Charlie's tales published as *Rawhide Rawlins* remembrances. Those volumes, first published as two softbound books in 1921 and 1925, respectively, were titled *Rawhide Rawlins* and *More Rawhides*. They each involved a method of anecdotal, oral storytelling delivered from a third-party perspective. In reviewing this manuscript, Chuck Rankin, retired editor-in-chief of the University of Oklahoma Press, was very much struck by how Nancy Russell was utilizing a similar approach in her biography of Charlie. It contains an eclectic array of vignettes bordering on stream of consciousness recollections drawn from three decades of her married life. The style of Nancy's biography of Charlie utilizes a rolling or unfolding narrative with topic headings, but without numbered chapters that would customarily provide a traditional organizational structure. Taken as a whole, it offers a fascinating combination of firsthand glimpses, insights, and perspectives.

In 1936, four decades after her marriage to Charlie and by then ten years widowed, Nancy was struggling to compose a memoir about her truly transformational thirty-year joint venture with the man who became widely known as the legendary "Cowboy Artist." John Taliaferro recounts in his 1996 Russell biography that following Charlie's death, Nancy embarked on a multi-year effort to have a biography published, hiring Dan Conway in 1927 to produce a manuscript. However, such an outcome was not to be. In what seems an abrupt dismissal of its publishability, Harry Maule of Doubleday judged it as offering "too much sentiment and not enough substance." Not one to be so easily put off, Nancy may have approached other publishers and been met with similar rejections. Taliaferro says, "After the debacle of the Conway biography, she also played with the idea of converting that flawed manuscript into her own memoir" and "She continued to work on her version of it right up to the end, but it was too much." Her reference herein to the "current war" (World War II) versus World War I (The Great War) confirms that she was still working on her manuscript in early 1940, merely a month or two prior to her death. Sadly, despite Nancy's determination, it proved to be too late for her to finish.

―――――

I purchased Nancy's unpublished manuscript about a decade ago from a retired pastor in Colorado Springs. He indicated that it and other Russell artifacts were gifts from the second husband of Helen Britzman. A widower, that individual inherited it from her estate along with various pieces of Russell furniture; clothing, including an elegant fur; and other personal items. The furniture and fur throw are now in the collection of the C.M. Russell Museum in Great Falls. Ms. Britzman's first husband, Homer Britzman, had purchased the manuscript along with much of the contents of Nancy Russell's home after her death and following the acquisition of important pieces of Russell art by C.R. Smith, then the CEO of American

Airlines. Thus, it seems that this document represents the working draft of Nancy's devoted efforts to develop her own account of what both she and Charlie affectionately called their life in "double harness."

It is understandable that today's reader might agree with the view of a publisher more than ninety years ago that Dan Conway's proposed biography on Charlie had more sentimentality than substance in it. Perhaps the same could be said of Nancy Russell's biography of her husband. Yet in an age when almost anything relating to Charlie Russell and his art has value to both collectors and scholars, and often firsthand insights are deemed priceless, I believe that Nancy Russell's biographical memoir merits being made available in book form to a wider audience. To be sure, some disjointedness of the stories being recounted remains evident. There are passages that reflect Nancy's memories of Charlie's recollections with all that implies about room for interpretation or error. For example, Nancy's recollection of Charlie's "night hawk" story about a moonlight scene involving Piegan Indian horse thieves moving through the Judith Basin with recently acquired Crow "wealth" triggered this writer's conclusion that it was likely the germ of the idea for his wonderfully accomplished 1901 oil, *The Horse Thieves*. That may or may not be correct, and we won't ever know for certain. But if it is not, I plead guilty to making a reasonable speculative leap. In any case, the story told to Nancy, and now us, as well as others like it, exemplifies the depth and authenticity of Charlie's cowboy days along with actual Indian encounters that inspired and informed so much of his artistic output.

Occasionally, observations seem to be thin or without much weight. In such cases, Nancy's recall can be limited and this is not always fully resolved. This is particularly true in the sections regarding Charlie's early years where she is recapturing her memory of his personal musings and feedback from other family members that are typically decades-old recollections. Nevertheless, what still comes through are often touching incidents such as those revealing his parents' dealings with his rebellious and truant boyhood. As the story of Charlie's ultimate move far to the north westward into Montana unfolds, the narrative strengthens noticeably.

For added perspective, Nancy is often relying on her own memory versus Charlie's, and she is running out of stamina. Whereas Charlie was also a skilled raconteur, especially by the 1920s, Nancy was not as practiced at storytelling. Furthermore, she is an aging Nancy whose vitality is waning by the late 1930s when she is still working on this book.

To be fair, by the early 1930s Nancy had accomplished much toward her goal of broadening the appreciation of Russell's art as well as his outlook on life. She had further promoted the *Rawhide Rawlins* genre by reconfiguring a number of those stories first presented in two softcover volumes as well as a few new ones into an improved hardcover book titled *Trails Plowed Under*, still in print today. She then developed the idea for *Good Medicine*, which showcased Charlie's humor, values, and philosophy of life via her extraordinary effort to promote a much-broadened availability of many of his legendary illustrated letters.

It is not surprising that Nancy's musings in a less-than-well-organized format would not get traction among Depression-era publishers in New York. To improve the flow of the narrative, the periodic randomness of Nancy's recollections has been rearranged into a more logical chronological order of events in this volume. I especially appreciate Brian Dippie's masterful contribution to this much improved sequencing. Her misspellings (that occasionally rival the amusing hallmark of Charlie's illustrated letters) have generally not been corrected unless it was critical to clarifying a point made. Otherwise, maintaining the manuscript as originally written has been the priority in order to convey the essence of Nancy Russell's story; that is, to preserve Nancy's voice to the greatest extent.

Notwithstanding the manuscript's shortcomings, Nancy's unpublished biography of Charlie Russell has redeeming merit. It offers fresh insights with a unique perspective. Charlie Russell personally witnessed the late stages and aftermath of an expanded, unfenced (open range) cattle industry. He observed its impact and that of other elements of westward expansion on the Plains Indian culture. His art essentially documented important historical changes underway in the buffalo-centric way of life of Native Americans and gave us dramatic interpretations of what he termed "the west that has passed." Whatever her limitations, his widow's compilation of Russell's empathetic perspectives on a variety of Indian tribes, including among others the Blackfeet, the Crow, the Cree, and the Assiniboine, are informative. Similarly, we can benefit from Nancy's firsthand account of Charlie's special friendships with Brother Van (Rev. W.W. Van Orsdel), Will Rogers, John

Matheson, Ben Roberts, William S. Hart, and such artists as Will Crawford, John Marchand, Ed Borein, and John Young-Hunter.

Finally, the manuscript provides a fascinating window into the nature of Charles and Nancy Russell's Western art enterprise. To test this line of thought, I asked Russell scholars Brian Dippie and Rick Stewart to examine it and render their perspectives about its utility as a valid source for C.M. Russell research inquiry. Brian agreed that various parts of it do provide new and useful perspectives, for example regarding the Russells' six-week trip to London and Paris in 1914 and a trip to Saskatoon in 1919. On this and other observations Rick Stewart concurred.

While reading the manuscript many times over the years, I have been repeatedly impressed with how frequently Nancy's writing correlates both directly, and periodically with intriguing indirectness, to circumstances and events influencing the genesis of ideas for Russell's artistic output. Accordingly, linking specific Russell images to Nancy's observations and timeline can provide enhanced insight into the likely inspiration for Charlie's art and subject matter development. In turn this deepens our appreciation of his talent and artistic process. Furthermore, when relevant comments can be included, benefiting from the more focused scholastic attention on the works of C.M. Russell in recent decades, especially by Brian Dippie, the late Peter Hassrick, Dr. Larry Len Peterson, Rick Stewart, Joan Carpenter Troccoli, Thomas Brent Smith, Karen McWhorter, and Laura Fry, this document becomes an even more enjoyable read.

I was delighted to discover that including images of a number of Charlie Russell paintings and sculptures serve to meaningfully augment Nancy's narrative. When combined with our commentary, it is intended that these compositions will infuse context and strengthen connection to the story Nancy is telling here. Whatever the merit of our endeavor, it represents our heartfelt tribute of special respect to Nancy Russell's worthy efforts to memorialize her remembrance of her husband, which can now stand fulfilled. The goal was achieved in no small part because of Brian Dippie's valuable contributions to this book as my fully committed collaborator. His unmatched (indeed, encyclopedic) knowledge of the intricacies of the Russell story and legacy has enormously elevated the final product, for which I am deeply grateful.

Prefatory Note
by Brian W. Dippie

NANCY COOPER RUSSELL knew Charles Marion Russell exactly half of his life. Born on March 19, 1864, he died on October 24, 1926, at the age of sixty-two years. She first met him in Cascade, Montana, in 1895, when he was thirty-one years old. For as long as she knew him he made his living as an artist. Everything she knew firsthand about him postdated his eleven years as a working cowboy and rested on memories—his and those of the people who knew him before she entered the picture. This should be kept in mind in reading her biography, written with the help of family and friends beginning in 1928, and never finished before her death on May 24, 1940, at sxity-two, the same age as Russell when he died. Half of her biography is what she heard or learned about the Cowboy Artist, half a personal account of their life together. Recognizing this, Nancy titled her biographical memoir "Back-Tracking in Memory: The Life of Charles M. Russell, Artist."

When Nancy died, she left behind an untitled manuscript—the basis of this book—as well as a stack of longhand drafts, hand-corrected typescript drafts, and a notebook. She also left several pages of notes she had jotted down about people and things she meant to cover in her book. They repose today in the Helen E. and Homer E. Britzman Collection—really, the Nancy Russell Estate Collection—at the Gilcrease Museum in Tulsa, Oklahoma. I have sifted through these papers to compare them to the typescript of Nancy's biographical memoir that Tom Petrie acquired about a decade ago. One hundred and sixteen pages long, the memoir lacks a foreword and an introductory chapter she had labored over without, apparently, satisfying her enough to include them with the rest of the manuscript in Tom's possession. She also left out the story of her first meeting with Charles Russell, having extracted it for publication in the biographical note that prefaced her collection of his illustrated letters, *Good Medicine* (1929). Its absence left a hole in the heart of her memoir. That meeting was a pivotal event in both their lives, and I have restored her full account of it and other material about Charlie's time in Cascade. These chapters flesh out Nancy's unfinished book, and thus have been incorporated into the text that follows, with the additions clearly identified.

Nancy made "Back-Tracking in Memory" a book about her husband and his work, not herself. Today we would welcome a chapter telling her own story before she met Charlie Russell in Cascade in 1895. She is fully present when she tells about their courtship and early years of marriage. We get a glimpse of the simple pleasures they shared as newlyweds that bonded them for life. She was willing to talk about the slights she endured and her wounded pride on a visit to a high-end dress shop in Paris, France; we would appreciate more such self-revelatory passages. Nancy planned to discuss their decision in December 1916, to adopt a three-month-old son, Jack Cooper Russell, but never got around to it. She left her book unfinished, but she never abandoned it entirely either. When a would-be Russell biographer contacted her in 1936 seeking her cooperation, she fended him off by stating, "I should like to read some of your published biographies as I have a strong feeling that the way you will put your material together will be so different from the way I am writing my story that they will not interfere with each other."

Indeed, as her biographical memoir took shape, she ignored strict chronology and adopted Charlie's storytelling technique of loosely connected yarns that bounced back and forth in time. That said, with her foreword now in place, her manuscript ends just where it should, on an open-ended anecdote about their life together trotting along in double harness, not without strains, as the foreword also makes clear, but as a team, artist and business manager, side by side forever.

When Joe De Yong, Charlie Russell's only artistic protégé, prepared an inventory of the Nancy Russell estate in February 1941, his final entry read: "Manuscript of Memoirs of Nancy C. Russell, together with all publication rights thereof." Through Tom Petrie's dedication to preserving the legacy of Charles Marion Russell, that manuscript has at last been published. It completes the trilogy of books Nancy had envisioned: a collection of Charlie's stories (*Trails Plowed Under*, 1927), a collection of his illustrated letters (*Good Medicine*, 1929), and a biography of "one of the greatest souls this country has ever known," *Back-Tracking in Memory: The Life of Charles M. Russell, Artist*—the book you now hold in your hands.

[Foreword]

*[Manuscript draft, Charles M. Russell Research Collection (Britzman),
Gilcrease Museum, Tulsa, OK, C.8.230]*

WILL ROGERS SAID, "He was a down right honest-to-God human being," which was true, and by my being the mouthpiece to back-track in memory of Charlie, quoting him as much as possible, the reader may get some of the thoughts of the real Charlie Russell and his philosophy.

He was not a business man. He knew absolutely nothing about the methods used in the business world, nor did he want to buy the food, pay the rent, or order coal. If we were going East, which was always against his wishes, he would not purchase the tickets or check the trunks. Room reservations and all the detail connected with exhibitions of or contracts for work disturbed and worried him. All those things were my job. It was a joy to supply his needs and do the things he could not do without disturbing his creative genius. It was much more important for him to record the history of the Great Northwest which was his work. . . .

HE WAS SURE HE WAS GOING TO BE
A GREAT EXPLORER LIKE WILLIAM BENT.

scene in the rocky mountians, from Charles M. Russell's Boyhood Sketchbook (ca 1878-79).
PETRIE COLLECTION.

Charlie's Boyhood Home

[Manuscript draft, Charles M. Russell Research Collection (Britzman), Gilcrease Museum, Tulsa, OK, C.8.230]

OAK HILL, [MISSOURI, WAS] an old-fashioned, comfortable country place. The house was large and rambling, the high-ceilinged rooms hung with life-size portraits of two generations of the Russell family and many fireplaces added charm. Hospitality was a creed and conversation an art. A full understanding of human worth flowed through those halls and surrounded the Russells, who for generations had lived in them. Visitors were not callers but welcome guests taken into the heart of the family. Such was the boyhood home of Charles M. Russell, who was born in the City of St. Louis on March 19th, 1864, but who spent most of his early childhood on the farm south of Tower Grove Park, Oak Hill, just out of St. Louis.

He was a born dreamer. A portrait of William Bent, his father's first cousin, always fired his imagination, and while standing in front of it, this towheaded boy could see himself in buckskin and long hair fighting Indians and conquering the West. He was sure he was going to be a great explorer like William Bent.

As a child, Charlie was a regular mother's boy, always close to her whenever in the house, sitting on her lap or, after he got too big for that, he would stand beside her with his arm around her neck. He was always sensitive to beauty and felt his brother Ed's golden head was much better looking than his, although the two boys were like twins. The family did not realize how Charlie felt until one day his mother found him standing on a chair before a mirror and heard him say, wistfully, "I don't think I'm so awful ugly, but my nose is hilly." The mother's love was returned in full by this small boy. She was a brilliant story-teller and saw joy and humor in life and could make others see it. Charlie inherited that talent from her.

Charlie's father had a wonderful way of talking and reading to his children and much of his time was spent with the six of them—one girl Sue, the eldest, and five boys, Bent, Charlie, Edward, Guy and Wolford [Wolfert].

HIS SHOULDER WHICH WAS BLACK AND BLUE FROM THE KICK

a stump or log 4 so of corse he
packed the ammunition an don most
of the loding we were shooting in turns
at evry thing in sight
well I kept belly aking saying my turn
an the big kid
sayig youl get
yours an I did
when he
loded for me
I remember
how the rod
jumped clear
of the barel
he spent five
or more minutes tamping
the loade
then handing the gun to me said thair
That would kill a tiger an I think it
would if hed been on the same end I was

Letter to Albert Trigg, November 10, 1903 (pg. 4), Charles M. Russell.
C.M. RUSSELL MUSEUM, GREAT FALLS, MONTANA, GIFT OF THE JOSEPHINE TRIGG ESTATE (953-1-054).

Charlie vividly recalled his bruising childhood experience on a visit to St. Louis in 1903.

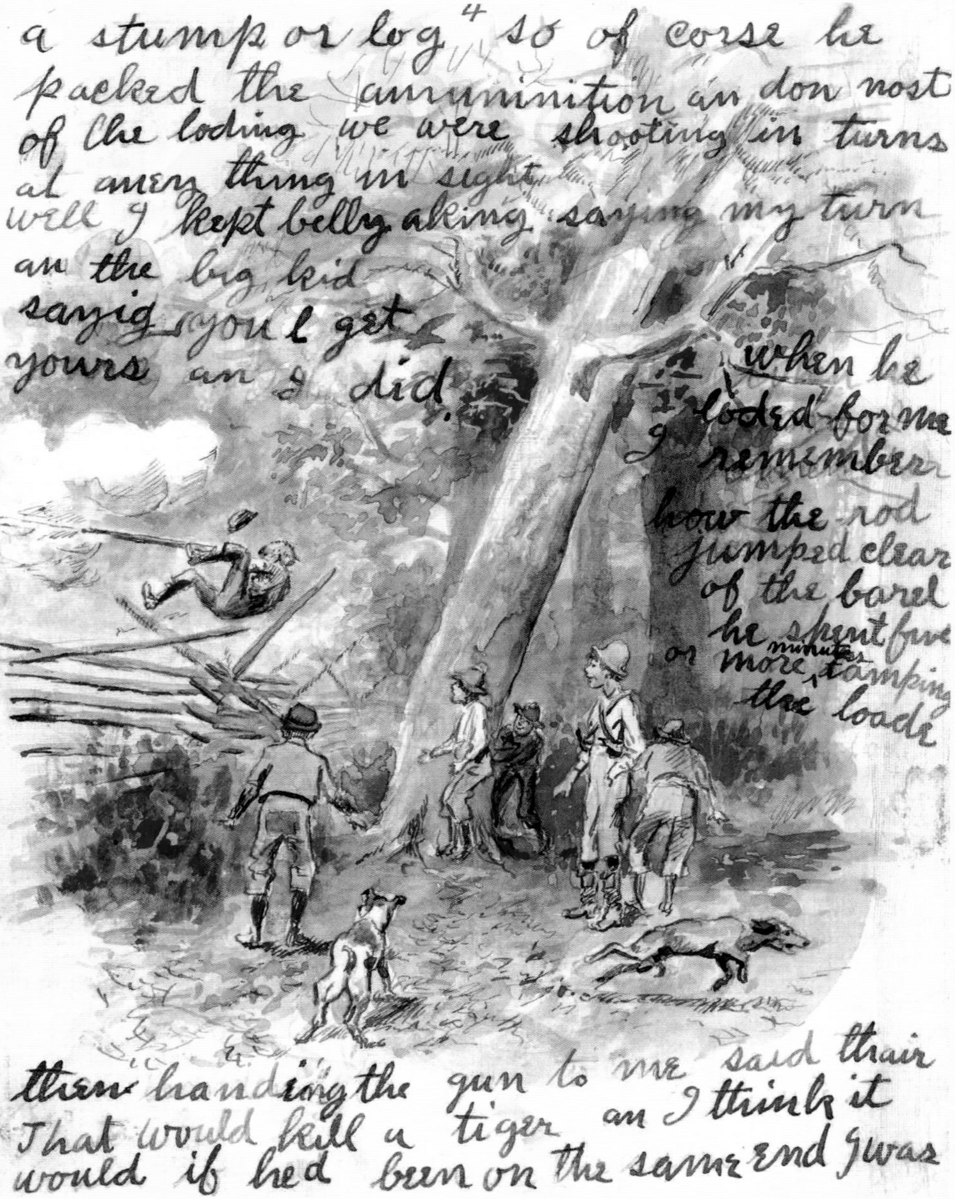

Someone asked Charlie if he remembered the little stone house. "Oh yes, it was like the mammoth cave to me, but it was only the milk house and I can see the wine house, as it was called, where apple cider and grape juice, sweet and fermented, was put up for the use of the family.["] In there were bins filled with sweet potatoes and apples—hard, juicy, wartie russets. Of course, there was a garden, an orchard, a vineyard, a pasture for the horses and cows, also stables, sheds, chicken houses and servants cabins built near by of black walnut logs; also a smoke-house where hams and bacons hung in the dim light, after the smoke had gone. The washout or gully lying between Oak Hill and Uncle George's [George Parker's], was like the Grand Canyon of the Colorado to him. They had caves there and the woods that his boy-mind made into a jungle. This was the finest kind of a place to scalp sister Sue's dolls.

Back of the orchard, these few acres of natural woods made an ideal place for children. Sometimes, when there were visiting youngsters, at the Russell home, Charlie and his dog, Tige, would lead the way back to the shadows of the trees where, in imagination, they heard bear and almost saw wolves. This was Grandpa's woods and they were sure scarey in the minds of those young warriors. They would play massacre and bedeck themselves in chicken and turkey feather war bonnets, clay for paint and bows and arrows; then steal the dolls, scalp them and burn them at the stake, just as they imagined their red-skinned brothers would do.

There were, as usual, one or two boys that had to be killed in the fight or if it was a make-believe bear or buffalo hunt, those same boys had to be "the meat". Charlie's imagination usually kept him from these parts, because he could plan the attack so well.

Sometimes their expeditions would be for game such as squirrels. One time, his older brother, Bent, was the leader and had an old gun that the boys took turns shooting. Their route was across a stubble field. The boys were barefooted. Charlie had tender feet, so could hardly keep up. Every time he would catch the boys, he would be saying, "When's my turn comin' to shoot?"

At last, Bent got tired of his whining and said, "You'll get your turn all right!" then started to load the gun. She was a muzzle-loader and he rammed the wad so tight, the ramrod almost bounced out of the barrel. When ready, he handed the gun to Charlie and said, "There, see if you can hit some of them crows over thar!"

Charlie said Bent was a real desperado when he was about ten years old and if he could think of it, would talk like he thought the old trappers did.

They were close to a rail fence, so Charlie climbed up, stood on next to the top rail, leaning his shins against the top, raised old trusty and fired at a bunch of crows. There was a loud report of powder exploding and a squeal from a young hunter. Charles had been kicked clear off the fence and landed all spraddled out but hanging on to the gun! He was through for that day. There was no damage done except to his shoulder which was black and blue from the kick.

Parker and Russell Families

THE PARKER AND RUSSELL FAMILIES were manufacturers of firebrick and gas retorts. West of the farm were coal and clay mines and a general store which were owned and managed by the Parker-Russell Firebrick Company. Most of their workmen were Irish and Welsh. Charlie was a favorite of their settlement and always welcome, for they loved this son of their boss.

During one visit Charlie was watching an old "Tarrier" dig a well. After answering some of the boy's questions, the old man asked, "Do ye smoke, my boy?"

"Aw, shore!" was the answer.

"Will ye kape me pipe a-goin' while I'm loadin't the buckets?"

The small boy sat on the pile of dirt and puffed away at the old dudeen. By the time Mike came out of the hole, a very white-looking little boy just sat holding the pipe, which had gone out.

"There's something the matter with me today, Mike. I couldn't keep her goin'."

"Not sick, are ye, Charlies? I thought you had a stout stumick."

"I have. It's my head. Maybe I'm getting measles. I guess I'd better go home."

Mrs. Hannah, another of his staunch friends, ran the country store. There was a big stove in the middle of the room with the dirt box under it. On the counters and against the wall were buckets of gumdrops and lemon drops, as well as peppermint sticks and small kegs of ginger snaps.

The store was a hang-out for Charlie.

"That's a fine stove you got, Mrs. Hannah. How long you had it?"

"Let me see—we bought it second-hand when the store was first opened, and that's about twenty-five years ago."

"It's sure fine," said Charlie, "and it keeps the place so nice and warm."

Then he would start looking around, until Mrs. Hannah would say, "Here, Charlie, are some gumdrops and ginger snaps for you."

He never forgot the taste of the things he talked Mrs. Hannah out of on those visits.

Jip and Tige

CHARLIE WAS EIGHT YEARS OLD when his father gave him a pony that he named "Jip," and from that time on, Charlie was never without a saddle horse. His pony and dog, Tige, were in on a lot of secrets. They were always connected with the hope of escape from school and [leading up to his ultimate goal] the journey West.

Each of the children had an allowance. Charlie saved his and did all the odd jobs he could to earn money. Father thought Charles would grow into an ordinary business man, for he seemed to be on the look-out for work that would pay.

The County Fair offered a cash prize for the best piece of modeling exhibited. In clay Charlie made a bas relief of a knight mounted, both man and horse armoured. It won first prize in the amateur class.

One day Charlie's room underwent a thorough cleaning. All the papers in the bureau were changed, and in one drawer, under the paper his mother found sixty dollars.

When she asked him about it, he replied, "Oh, I wanted that to go West on!"

The money was put in the bank for him, but as far as Charlie was concerned, it was gone. He did not know how to get it and would not ask for it.

A Visit to
Father's Reading Room

FATHER WAS IMPATIENT, and the children worried [frustrated] him with their noisy play when he tried to read, unless he was reading to them, which he did for an hour almost every night. He read the "Frank Stories," and histories of Crockett, Boone and Kit Carson. All of these the boys adored.

But there were times when Father wished to read his own books. Then he said, "I'm going to build a library for myself, and you children have got to stay out of there!"

When the room was finished, the five boys were of course there under foot. The room was small; Charlie was squeezed in at the end of Father's desk. This was before the days of electricity, and a fancy [gas-fired] bracket lamp hung low so that the light would shine on the desk and the reading chair. Charlie, wriggling around between chair and desk, rose up under the lamp. The fancy iron pricked a hole in his scalp.

Charlie let out a howl, whereupon Father scattered them all, saying, "What business had you in there? It's good enough for you! Now maybe you will stay out. This is my room—not meant for you boys. Now get out and stay out of here!"

Next evening Father was again reading in his study. This time Charlie was seated on the floor, modelling green and pink horses out of [wax] what Sister Sue had left from making flowers. He used sticks for legs and paint brushes for tails. Everything was quiet and peaceful until Father dropped a piece of his paper and in stooping over for it raised up under the same sharp iron on the new lamp.

This time it was different! Father cried, "A man should be shot who would make such a murderous thing!" He didn't see why traps like that were set for honest men. Then he turned to his wife. "Mary, that damned thing must be moved before it hurts somebody!"

Charlie crept out of the room, for he was laughing, and it would not do for his father to see a smile on anybody's face but Mother's.

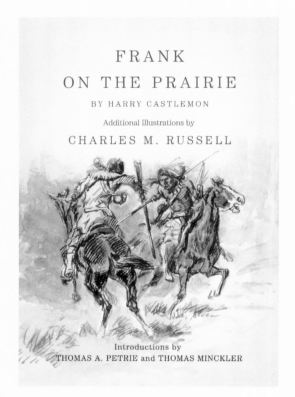

FRANK
ON THE PRAIRIE

BY HARRY CASTLEMON

Additional Illustrations by

CHARLES M. RUSSELL

Introductions by
THOMAS A. PETRIE and THOMAS MINCKLER

Frank on the Prairie by Harry Castlemon (Philadelphia: Henry T. Coats & Co., 1893).
Extra-illustrations by Charles M. Russell (1903).
PETRIE COLLECTION.

At another time Father was perched on a step-ladder, mending something. He had been using a hammer and was ready for it again. It could not be seen. He turned to the ever-present children. "Now, which of you young rascals took that hammer? I want it—and quick!"

There was a scattering that took all the boys but Charlie out of the room. He stood still a few seconds, then whispered something to his mother and disappeared with a giggle. Father was sitting on the hammer, and nobody but Mother dared tell him!

Charlie modelled with any material he could find that his small fingers could press into form. Among some pictures he found a [magazine] cut of an American eagle which he liked, but he wanted the eagle to have a rabbit in its claws for the little eagles that could not [yet] get out of the nest [for food]. When the model was finished, Charlie printed the exact words which were under [the] original pictures: "copyright reserved."

To his mother's question, "What's that, Charlie?" the boy replied, "Oh, don't you know? That's his name."

Frank on the Prairie by Harry Castlemon was one of the "Frank Stories" most probably read by Charles Silas Russell to his children in the early to mid-1870s. It was among the author's first four volumes that ultimately totaled forty-two separately published boys' adventure tales. Some thirty years later, in 1903, Charlie noticed that his nephew Austin Russell, son of his brother Bent, was reading this same book. Russell borrowed that copy and extra-illustrated it with eleven original watercolors and one pencil drawing that served to bring the characters and plot alive. The story itself closely mirrors events detailed in Francis Parkman's 1849 classic, *The Oregon Trail*. It involves similar experiences of two teenage boys shortly after the Civil War guided by an uncle and a frontiersman along that same basic route. In 2017, the C.M. Russell Museum published a new edition of *Frank on the Prairie* complete with high-resolution images of the stirring Russell art.

Charlie Russell as a young boy, photographer unknown.
C.M. RUSSELL MUSEUM, GREAT FALLS, MONTANA.

Charlie's Golden
Curls are Cut

THE RUSSELL FAMILY often visited their relatives in Virginia. During one of these stays in Winchester when Charles was about five years old, the elderly Irish nurse was watching the children play in a public park where a small stream ran through mud banks. This was the place Charlie liked to stop and make things out of the clay. He did his best to scare the nurse with his creations. That day he fashioned a coiled snake. The nurse pretended to be much frightened.

While they were playing, an elderly gentleman stopped to ask Charlie where he had got the wicked reptile.

Charlie said the snake came all the way from the jungle to bite Mollie but "I am going to kill him before he hurts her very much."

Then two little feet jumped on the clay and mashed the snake flat.

The gentleman was interested in Charlie, whom he had seen modelling other bits in the mud. He praised the boy's work and asked to be introduced to his father.

When the two men met, the stranger knew that Charlie's father had the means and the desire to encourage Charlie to study whatever was best for him.

The stranger said, "This boy has a good deal of talent. He should go to an art school." And he patted Charlie's head and spoke of those curls which his mother so loved—and which Charlie hated!

It was like a girl's hair. All his begging to have it cut short was to no avail. Poor little Charlie had been put off from week to week.

But the very next day after the stranger's visit a fine chance came to get rid of the offending curls. As usual, the nurse took the children past the spot in the park where workmen were busy with repairs. There Charlie's alert eye discovered a barrel of tar open for use.

Remembering his desperate but futile efforts to get his curls cut, he slipped away while no attention was being paid to him. And he busily patted tar all over his hair.

This maneuver was a great success. Not only did the curls have to be cut, but his head had to be shaved.

Mother thought Father should do something about this, but Father said, "Mary, I don't blame Charlie. I think he was pretty smart to [figure out how to] get rid of his curls."

detail from a letter from C.M. Russell to Charles M. Street, in *Your Friend, C.M. Russell*,
THE C.M. RUSSELL MUSEUM COLLECTION OF ILLUSTRATED LETTERS

Charlie received more than his fair share of blame and punishment.

Very often he was unjustly whipped.

Smothered by Routine

SINCE OAK HILL WAS SO FAR OUT in the country, the children had to be taken to and from school. A large carriage held the children, cousins and all. They were taken each morning, [from] near their various homes and then picked up after school.

Any confinement always was a horror to Charlie. Teachers did not bother to find out what he really could do and, because he could not be made to study out of books, he was punished a good deal in those days.

The teachers were usually men, and Charlie hated them. So he spent most of his time trying to avoid the routine of school.

There was one teacher he never forgot. Every time anything went wrong in the room, Charlie received more than his share of blame and punishment. Very often he was unjustly whipped, so the boys got together and agreed that the next time a boy was called up for a whipping that he did not deserve they would double up on the teacher and show that he had to be square [i.e., fair].

The teacher's desk was on a platform. He was in the habit of leaning his chair back against a closed door that led down three steps to a storeroom. With his chair tipped, he would cover his eyes with his hands and watch the pupils through his fingers.

He was on guard this way one day soon after the boys had made their plan of defense. One of the boys did something for which he was called to the platform for the strap. After the first whack, Charlie stood up and called, "Come on, fellers!"

He started for the teacher. But not another boy stirred. There were two boys instead of one who got the strap—the last, much harder than usual.

Charlie, determined to get even with that teacher, knew he must do it alone.

He could not work out of those books; his very heart and soul were being crushed and hardened by the rules of a regular school into which he was unable to fit himself. He drew pictures on the margins of his books; he was thereupon punished for mutilating them instead of studying from them.

The young boy was indeed being smothered by rules and routine. The fire

HE DREW PICTURES ON THE MARGINS OF HIS BOOKS;
HE WAS THEREUPON PUNISHED FOR MUTILATING THEM
INSTEAD OF STUDYING FROM THEM.

THE WRECK OF THE PENOBSCOT.

CHAPTER V.

MONKEY.

Photographs accompanying "Childhood Works of Artist Charles Marion Russell Discovered,"
press release by the Missouri Historical Society, St. Louis, June 8, 1982.
BRIAN W. DIPPIE COLLECTION, VICTORIA, BC.

of genius burned in his soul. He did not understand it and could not explain it.

Finally he thought of a way to upset the teacher. This time, he went alone. The room was empty, so Charlie was able to unlock and unlatch the door back of the teacher's desk and pull it shut so that it looked as usual.

That afternoon a small boy was looking through his fingers, waiting for the teacher to take his chair and go on guard. He thought the teacher would never sit down, but at last he took his place and tilted the chair back. It hit the door, went on through and dumped the teacher head-first into a pile of old desks and chairs.

When he returned to the room, it was in war-like mood. Everyone had been laughing, but a deadly hush came over the pupils when they saw the expression on his face.

"Does anyone know who opened that door?"

Nobody said a word.

Charlie looked sorrier than anyone there—sorry, he later confessed, because the fall hadn't broken the teacher's neck! Thirty years later Charlie met that teacher and told him who set the trap.

He often played sick so that he could stay home from school. Soon after the carriage had gone, Charlie improved remarkably and had a grand time in Grandpa's woods for the rest of the day with his dog and pony.

When Father got on to that, it didn't work any more.

AT THAT TIME ST. LOUIS WAS THE LARGEST
MULE MARKET IN THE WORLD.

Corralling Mules, from Charles M. Russell's Boyhood Sketchbook (ca 1878-79).
PETRIE COLLECTION.

This is likely a scene Charlie experienced on his truancy-inspired visits to the St. Louis docks. It is interesting to note that as a young teenager Charlie is signing his work with his CMR initials along with a moccasin symbol. Much later he replaces that with a full C.M. Russell signature and the buffalo skull.

Charlie Plays Hookey

CHARLIE HAD A FRIEND, Archie [Douglass] by name, who later graduated with honors from one of the best colleges in the country and has been a very successful business man. These two stayed together. They invented an excuse for Charlie to miss school, saying that he was going to visit an aunt in Kirkwood and would be gone for some time. Archie wrote it, because he could write better than Charlie. They got away with this ruse for seven weeks, and Charlie played hookey.

Each morning he took his books and rode with the other children to the corner. But instead of going on to school, he hid his books and went on down to the river front or to the levees or the mule markets. There he talked to the negroes loading and unloading the river boats.

And he listened, absorbed, to the fur traders, retaining all he heard about the great Northwest. He knew he was going there some day—but how?

At that time St. Louis was the largest mule market in the world. Uncle Sam bought by the hundreds, as did railway companies and independent freighters that were drifting west. At times there was a great clatter over the cobblestones as bands or strings of mules were moved from one place to another. The jingle of bells and the call of the drivers were sweet music to the ears of the little boy.

Maybe he could join one of these outfits some time!

After several weeks of this vacation, Archie said to Charlie, "You better come back to school or you're sure to get caught!"

Although Archie had already gone back to school, Charlie thought his freedom too good to give up. He said, "Aw, I'll be back some time. But not yet."

He was well into the seventh week of his holiday when one evening he was walking toward the corner where the carriage always called for the children. He was a little ahead of time. His gaze seemed to be drawn to the school—and there, coming straight toward him, was his father.

He had been to the school and knew everything. Charlie could tell from the way his father walked what was going to happen to him, but he stood still.

When his father reached him, he said in a low voice, "Son, go home. I will attend to you there!" and walked on past without another word.

Charlie was certain something awful would happen. He knew he deserved it. He did not know why he had done the dreadful thing—including using his mother's name without her knowing it. He was sure they would send him to prison for life; they might even hang him. He would rather be whipped than have his father talk to him as he knew he would. He could just see where he would wind up if he went on the way he was going. His father had warned him, but this was going to be much worse.

Well, he just could not go home. He was an eleven-year-old, an outlaw—and he might as well act like one!

He left his books under the sidewalk where they were cached and went back to the mule market, hoping to find someone who was going west and would take him along. His money was still in the bank, and since he couldn't get it, his only hope was to work for some of these men westward bound.

"No, son, there ain't no outfits pullin' tonight, but you can sleep in the hay here, and maybe there'll be somethin' doin' tomorrow."

At dusk one of the men gave him a new horse blanket and told him to crawl in the hay. Charlie had never gone to sleep without saying his prayers, but this was no time for prayers because he was too bad even to think of God. The hay and the blanket were all right, and he was not too hungry. Yet sleep would not come. Those prayers kept worrying him.

Just before he fell asleep, he was thinking, "It won't be any use for God to try to take care of me, but please bless Jip and Tige, Mother, Father and oh, everybody at home."

Though he stayed around the stables for three days, there was no chance to start West. Some of the men persuaded him to go home and wait until he grew big enough to handle mules by himself.

A man who lived south of the city took him as far as his place, and Charlie walked the rest of the way home. The family, worried over his disappearance, had not been able to find any trace of him. They were overjoyed to see him—it was like the Prodigal's return—and for the time nothing was said about the trick that had kept him from school.

However, he was not sent back to school but had lessons at home with a young Episcopal minister, a Mr. Chestnut, who had just taken the Mission Church in their neighborhood.

CHARLIE LOVED THE FRANK BOOKS [DESCRIBED PREVIOUSLY]
AND DID HIS DESPISED LESSONS IN ORDER TO DRIFT
IN IMAGINATION WITH HIS HEROES.

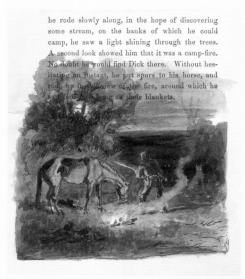

he rode slowly along, in the hope of discovering some stream, on the banks of which he could camp, he saw a light shining through the trees. A second look showed him that it was a camp-fire. No doubt he would find Dick there. Without hesitating an instant, he put spurs to his horse, and rode up in full view of the fire, around which he saw four men lying on their blankets.

Black Bill

198   FRANK ON THE PRAIRIE.

THE travelers had been intensely interested in the old trapper's story, and not even the thought that the danger was passed, and that Frank was safe in camp again, could altogether quiet their feelings. Frank was more astonished than ever, and he secretly determined

Frank on the Prairie by Harry Castlemon (Philadelphia: Henry T. Coats & Co., 1893).
Extra-illustrations by Charles M. Russell (1903).
PETRIE COLLECTION.

Additional *Frank on the Prairie* adventures and episodes include a buffalo stampede that results in being lost on the prairie and a holdup by a bad gang that necessitates capturing and training a wild horse. One can readily see how young Charlie's yearning to go west would be triggered by such experiences recounted in the Frank Stories.

A Try at Art School

WHEN HE ARRIVED HOME, he discovered that his father wanted him to go to art school. He had secured a tutor for his regular studies, and this arrangement worked far better.

When the weather permitted, studying was done in Charlie's beloved woods. Lessons would be learned so they could go exploring. They also read a good deal of history and frontier life. Charlie loved the Frank books [described previously] and did his despised lessons in order to drift in imagination with his heroes.

Art school sounded all right to Charlie. Father took him over [to it] the first day, found out and ordered what he needed in the way of working [art] materials. They learned that Charlie's class was from nine until twelve.

The family had moved for the winter into St. Louis to the house where Charlie had been born. It was not far from the art school. The arrangements seemed ideal.

But on the third day of school Charlie brought his modelling clay and drawing material home with him.

"What's up now?" asked Father.

"I'm through with art school," said Charlie firmly. His complaints were definite. The instructor has not time for a kid like me. He sets up a plaster foot and tells the class to draw it. I did. Then he came around me, he'd say, 'It won't do,' so I'm through."

That was the only art school Charlie ever attended. [While Russell did not take additional formal art lessons, in later years it became clear that he naturally absorbed and effectively adopted many tips, insights, and techniques garnered from numerous artist friends on trips to St. Louis, New York, London, California, and elsewhere, including visits by artist friends to Montana.]

[Years later] He said Nature had been his teacher and would leave it to the world whether or not she had done a good job. He also said to have talent was no credit to its owner, for what a man can't help he should have neither praise nor blame, for it is not his fault.

He was thinking, watching, planning for the chance to go West. Archie was to go with him this time; they had made all their plans. They were going to take Jip and Tige and take turns riding. Archie would furnish the grub and Charlie the horse and dog.

When they finally did start, neither family knew about it. And between them they had two loaves of bread and eight dollars in money.

The first night out they slept in a haystack and let the pony graze. It was early summer. The weather was pleasant, so their hay bed was fine.

About sun-up, they were awakened by the owner of the hay, to whom they explained that they were going West. After suggesting that he could use a couple of likely boys if they wanted to work, he took them to the house and gave them breakfast.

Oh, no, they could pay for their food, and they were going to join a fur trader out West. They must be on their way.

At noon Archie wondered if it wouldn't have been better to stay at the farm and join a big outfit going to the far West. Charlie disagreed. He had waited over a year for that start, so he was going on.

Again they slept in the hay—this time in a barn. Again the owner gave the boys supper—plenty of milk, with which the boys ate the last of their bread. They had spent part of their eight dollars.

Just at daylight the boys were pulled out of the hay and told to wash if they wanted breakfast. The man was milking. Soon a bell called them to the house. The two adventurers wet their faces at the horse trough, and the air dried them. Their hair, though dampened too, would not lie down with their patting—one a brick-red, and other a tow-head.

After breakfast the farmer asked them to work for him. There was corn to be hoed, he told them, tobacco to be suckered and the garden to be cultivated. Charlie was for going on, but Archie said he was sick and he wanted to go home.

So they separated.

Archie went back to St. Louis, and Charlie stayed with the farmer, keeping his pony and dog with him. Archie had all the money, and Charlie must earn some for himself before he could go on.

He stayed three months. He said later that he never knew anyone could burn so much wood as the farmer's wife did. He had to split it for her and keep a supply in the kitchen. It would fade away like mist. But he had to have that money, and this was the only way to get it—to stay with his job.

At the end of the three months he had saved every possible cent. The total was not very imposing—just eleven dollars and a half. Four dollars and thirty-five cents of the precious money went for shoes, pants and shirts.

He had tried to learn to milk but pinched the cow, and she kicked him over. He said if they could have found a way to turn her upside down so that he could get at the faucets, he might have stolen some of the milk from the calf, for after all, that was the one to whom it belonged.

The things he could do were coming to an end. The garden had been opened and gathered; the corn was ready to harvest, but they needed for this man who knew his work. Unless Charlie did better and learned something, he would have to go.

Since he wasn't interested in farming and couldn't get the hang of things, it seemed best for him to go home for a while and try to join a big outfit headed for the Northwest.

He remembered how glad the family had been to see him when he had been away that first time. He was sure it would be even better this time, as he had been gone so long.

The dog, the pony and boy turned back toward Oak Hill. There they arrived about supper time. All the family were home.

Charlie put his horse in the pasture, hung up his saddle and, with Tige yapping in front of him, went to the house.

His family said "Howdy", just as if he had been out playing. They showed no surprise or joy at his return. He was told that he had better get a pail of water and then clean up for supper.

This home-coming was not at all what he had expected!

He found out later that Archie had betrayed his whereabouts. Father, trying to drive him home and [back] to school, had paid the farmer to keep him and work him just as hard as he could.

After he had crawled into bed that first night, his mother came to see if there was [bed] cover enough. She pushed the rebellious hair back from a very sad, troubled face, patted him and said, "Son, Mother had missed you, and she understands."

Her sympathy was too much. It opened the flood-gate, and the big little

I WILL DO ALL I CAN AND WILL NOT TRY TO KEEP YOU HERE,
EVEN THOUGH WE ALL THINK YOU SHOULD STAY.

Portrait of Mary Elizabeth Mead Russell (ca 1850-60), artist unknown.
C.M. RUSSELL MUSEUM, GREAT FALLS, MONTANA (S991.19.678).

This second homecoming incident is revealing of Mary Mead Russell's vital role as
Charlie's anchor for emotional support in his early truancy-troubled boyhood. In addi-
tion, an artist herself, she has often been credited with providing encouragement of
Charlie's artistic inclinations.

boy sobbed his heart out to his mother and told her for the first time in a way that she understood that he must get to the open West some way! If they didn't send him, he would keep running away and trying until he did get there.

"We will [see] what can be done, but Son, you must tell Mother next time before you start. I will do all I can and will not try to keep you here, even though we all think you should stay."

A Dream of Burlington (1880), Charles M. Russell.
PETRIE COLLECTION.

A Dream of Burlington is one of Russell's first works of art executed after settling in Montana. It depicts Charlie sleeping in what most likely was Babcock's cabin in the Judith Basin. Old Bab was a unique character and special friend of Russell's described later in Charlie's letter to Brother Van Orsdel (pages 43–46). In his dreams shown here, Charlie is recalling his trials at the military school. These include a "running the gauntlet," a traditional Indian harassment technique; cadets marching many hours of simulated guard duty as punishment to work off his excessive demerits; and a paddle wheeler passing a George Caleb Bigham–type river barge, apparently referencing a sight Charlie saw on the long one-way trip home to St. Louis via the Ohio River.

He Goes to Burlington College

When Charlie was fourteen [fifteen], his father sent him to Burlington College, a military school which Charlie's friend, Archie Douglas[s], [also] attended at Burlington, New Jersey.

Father told Charlie that if he would stay and work through that term, when he came home he would be allowed to go West, if he still wanted to.

With this in mind, Charlie's sole purpose was to get through that term as quickly as possible in order to go West.

The boys were rewarded for good behavior by a trip up to Philadelphia on the Saturday boat. Charlie went the first Saturday but was [confined to] campus every week-end thereafter, deficient in all his studies but history. He often said later that he doubted if he would ever have learned to read if it had not been for [the incentive provided by] Ned Buntline's dime novels.

Many times he would have one of these hidden inside his geography book and was just at the point where the villain was about to get the girl, when the teacher thumped him on the head, took his story and destroyed it, so Charlie never knew what happened to that girl. He supposed that the villain got the worst of it and the good boy won the girl.

Those memories never left him. They were not funny to him, nor did he forgive the various teachers who had such difficulty in getting him to do some book work. His instructors wondered why he came there at all. One even went so far as to say, "Charlie, you grieve me to the heart."

As punishment he walked guard for hours, carrying a wooden gun. [This is depicted in the right center of *A Dream of Burlington*.] On these occasions he imagined himself a Texas ranger or a scout, protecting some wagon trains from the Redskins, or he was one of Kit Carson's friends going to Fort Bent to trade [with his great uncles who built and operated that famous fort on the Santa Fe Trail].

When school was dismissed for the summer vacation, Charlie had over one hundred hours that he was supposed to walk before he would go. His father had sent his ticket to come home. He followed the other boys aboard the train and waved good-bye to the captain from the observation platform.

They were probably very glad to have him go!

The Jerk Line (1912), Charles M. Russell.
C.M. RUSSELL MUSEUM, GREAT FALLS, MONTANA, GIFT OF FRED BIRCH (959-5-1).

It is noteworthy that Nancy's detailed description of the freighters' teams along with the lash of the whip comport so closely with Charlie's composition *The Jerk Line*.

Leaving for Montana
1880

IN THE EARLY PART OF MARCH 1880, just before Charlie's sixteenth birthday, and after [even] more struggles with school that failed to [resonate or take] hold of him, Father said, "Charlie, there is a gentleman I know [named Pike Miller] who is going West. How would you like to go with him to Montana?"

Father was going to try another way. He knew what the answer would be and thought this fifteen-year-old son would be willing to come home in a short time to [again] take [up] the educational training awaiting him.

With Pike Miller, Charlie went by [the Union Pacific to the] Utah-Northern Railway, then by stage-coach to Helena, Montana. When they arrived there, the streets were lined with freight outfits. Bull teams with their dusty whackers, swinging a sixteen-foot lash with gunlike report over seven or eight yoke of bulls. The string of talk was profane, but it was understood by every bull. Mule skinners, as jerk-line men astride their saddle animals, jerked the line that led to the little span of leaders.

These teams were sometimes horses, sometimes mules, with twelve to fourteen span to the team, often pulling three wagons chained together, the teams handled by one line.

It was also ration time for the Indians in that section, and the red men were standing or riding in that quiet way of theirs, all wearing skin leggings and robes. The heart of one youthful traveler was filled with the picturesqueness of the whole scene. He knew that he had found his country, the place he would make his home. But he could not know what a great part he was to take in recording its history, its very picturesqueness, for coming generations.

On the coach he managed to sit with the driver, so that he would not miss anything. There was an old fellow who asked, "where ye frum, Bud?"

Swelling with pride, Charlie told him. "Missouri."

The old person put his fingers to his lips. "Sh! Not so loud. Don't ever tell anybody you're frum there. I am, too, but I don't tell it, 'cause there's a tree in Helena that they use to hang Missourians on just as fast as they can

THEY HAD A HARD TIME CROSSING THE CRAZY MOUNTAINS,
FOR THE WAGON TRAILS WERE VERY DIM AND ROUGH,
AND ONE OF THE HORSES WAS PLAYED OUT.

When Wagon Trails Were Dim (1919), Charles M. Russell.
Albert K. Mitchell Collection, National Cowboy & Western Heritage Museum,
OKLAHOMA CITY, OKLAHOMA (1975.020.5).

cetch' em, so, son, come frum any other state, but never say Missouri where anybody can hear ye!"

At the stage station fresh horses were always ready to take the place of the weary ones. When meal time came, the passengers had but a few minutes to eat the food, which was plain but good. Meat—usually wild game—boiled beans, dried apples, sour dough bread and coffee roasted in the dutch oven. All the coffee came green. Everyone had mills in which to grind it fresh each meal, but they didn't always empty and clean the coffee pot. But how good the coffee tasted to the weary traveler, even if the pot was half full of stale grounds!

Any mention of coffee pots always reminded Charlie of a very grouchy fellow who had been sent with three other cow punchers to "rep" for their outfit.

The first night out they began to cook over their camp fire before they had made a good camp. One of the men put the coffee pot on. Just as it was about to boil, it tipped over, spilling over the bacon and on to the bank, and it almost put out the fire.

The coffee cook hastily jumped on the pot, then kicked it all 'round the camp. One of the other men cried, "Wait a minute!" He ran to his bed roll, grabbed his gun and shot the offending coffee pot full of holes with the words, "I won't allow no damned coffee pot to impose on a pardner of mine."

For the balance of that trip, they used an empty tomato can [to make coffee].

In Helena Mr. Miller outfitted, buying a wagon and four horses, two of them for Charlie. With their load of "grub" they then pulled out for Miller's sheep ranch in the Judith Basin country.

They had a hard time crossing the Crazy Mountains, for the wagon trails were very dim and rough, and one of the horses was played out.

Although they arrived at the ranch a very weary outfit, Charlie's mind was made up about driving a team and wagon. He often said later, "You can have a car if you want it and can learn to drive. I'm willing to water it, but don't ever ask me to do anything else to it." Pack and saddle horses were his favorite mode of transportation, and he never changed.

He stayed with Miller only a few weeks, as the sheep and Charlie did not get along at all well. He didn't think Miller missed him much, for the man considered him "ornery" and just a dreamer.

[Upon his dismissal and] With his two horses Charlie went to a stage station where he heard they needed a horse herder. But his dislike for the sheep

Charles M. Russell on Monty (or Monte), Utica (1886).
Photograph by Townley & Runsten, Mandan, D.T.
PETRIE COLLECTION.

Charles M. Russell as a Young Man (ca 1886),
photographer unknown. Gilcrease Museum,
TULSA, OKLAHOMA (TU2009.39.5667A).

As the picture on the right shows in greater detail, Charlie is wearing the same fringed and beaded deer hide jacket as he wore in the first picture. With this traditional attire, he became widely known across Montana as the "Buckskin Kid." That treasured jacket was kept by Charlie and then by Nancy throughout both their lives. It was among the prized items comprising Nancy's estate in 1940 in California. Thus, today it is part of the Britzman Archives at the Gilcrease Museum.

and his inability to hold the band [of them] had got there ahead of him. He found the men unwilling to entrust their horses to him.

He did not get the job. But destiny was guiding him.

Leading his pack horse, carrying a very light bed, Charlie "pulled" [out] for the Judith River. There he made camp and picketed his horses. He had a lot of thinking to do. As he unrolled his bed, a man's voice called out, "Hello, Kid! What are you doing here?"

"Camping."

"Where's your grub?"

"Haven't any."

"Where you going?"

"To find a job."

"Where you from?"

Charlie told the man, who said, "You better come over and camp with me; I got a lot of elk meat, beans and coffee. That ought to feel pretty good to the inside of a kid like you."

Indeed, it is strange how food given in the right spirit will change one's whole outlook on life.

That was the way Charlie [met] Jake Hoover, hunter and trapper, who became his life-long friend.

That night they camped together. At breakfast time Jake advised Charlie to get rid of his horses; they were a big team and one was a mare.

Jake told him, "This country is no place for a lady horse. If she took a notion, she would leave and take every other horse in the country with her, leaving us a-foot."

Charlie was to learn later that the mares are the real leaders. You might see a stallion head up, tail flagging, prancing around as if he owned the country, but when the horses wanted to change ranges or find new water, the mares led the way [much the same as a bull elk typically follows the elk cows].

Charlie said it was the same with human beings. In the trail ahead of man is a track the same shape as his—only smaller—a woman's foot-print. It may lead to heaven or hell, but he will follow.

[Given Jake's advice] In a few days they met a band of Piegan Indians with whom they traded [the mare] for two smaller horses, one a pinto that Charlie named Monty. They were like children together. [Over two decades later] When Monty died in 1904, Charlie had ridden and packed him thousands of miles. People who knew one knew the other, for they were inseparable. They didn't exactly talk, but they "savvied" each other. Monty was a real cow pony and, like his owner, did not care for sheep.

Once a band [of sheep] was crossing a range where the horses were grazing. Sheep scatter as they travel, and one of them came too near Monty. Monty grabbed it by the middle of its back with his teeth, striking both ends of the sheep a death blow with his front feet. Then—almost as a dog would do—Monty shook it, dropped it and walked away as if it were his right to dispose of sheep in that way.

Years later, Charlie needed some wood for the fire at his camp on the Dearborn [River]. The work horses were in a pasture some distance from camp. Since Monty was picketed nearby, Charlie thought, "I'll put the [horse collar] harness on him and he can drag in some wood."

When the rope was fastened to the log, Monty was led forward until the rope was taut and the [horse] collar was pressed against his shoulders. He stopped still and looked about him, as much as to say, "This is a work [i.e., draft] horse's job, and I won't do it!"

Then he quietly lay down, and the look in his eyes as he rolled them at Charlie said, "I will die rather than disgrace my position with you."

Charlie took off the harness, put his saddle on Monty, and with a rope and by the horn of his saddle, Monty dragged in all the wood needed for the camp without a moment's hesitation.

Monty was a cow pony again and would pull anything by the rope and horn of the saddle!

More About Jake Hoover

CHARLIE LIVED WITH JAKE HOOVER about two years. They had six horses: a saddle horse each and pack animals. They hunted and trapped, [occasionally even taking bighorn sheep], and selling bear, deer, and elk meat to the settlers as well as sending the furs and pelts in to Fort Benton to trade.

All during his life with Jake, Charlie studied the habits of all the different types of men and animals he knew, and he drew them. Living with a trapper, he got close to the hearts of the wild animals, seeing them in their own habitat and with their young, witnessing their struggle against their enemies—especially man.

Hoover would say, "Charlie, you're to get [to shoot] a deer today."

Soon they jumped a band of whitetail, for the country was alive with game. Charlie, shaking with excitement, shouted at the top of his voice, "Here they come! Here they come! There they go!" while he pumped every shell out of his gun without firing a shot. He never was a willful killer of wild game.

Years later he tried to hunt for pleasure. The deer stood within easy range; another hunter spoke softly, "Fire quick or I'll get him myself."

Charlie, with a sharp movement, not only dropped his gun but ruined the aim of his friend. "I cant' kill him," he said, "and I won't let you."

Hoover, too, was kind-hearted. He had traded some elk meat for a little pig which became a regular pet. One evening Jake announced, "The feed's run out, and it's time we should have some pork. In the morning we'll kill him."

Jake was up first, pulled on his boots and bellowed, "Come on, Kid, we'll do the dirty work, and then we'll eat."

Charlie said that he could see that Jake felt all wrong inside. As Jake went out, he picked up the ax. When he climbed the fence, the pig saw Jake and came running to rub its nose against the old trapper's leg.

"Get out! Get away from me! This ain' no friendly visit. Her[e] Kid," handing Charlie the ax, "you smash him—he's no friend of yours."

"No, I won't," Charlie came back. "You do your own killing."

THEY HUNTED
AND TRAPPED

Hunter's Rest (ca. 1892) harkens back to Charlie's formative hunting experiences with Jake Hoover. When viewing the bighorn sheep in this painting together with *Sentinel Duty* below, another watercolor of the same 1892 period, one can imagine how this could be the germ of an idea for his much later masterpiece, *Meat's Not Meat 'Till It's in the Pan* (page 39). It was executed some twenty-three years later by C.M. Russell in 1915.

Hunter's Rest (ca 1892), Charles M. Russell.
PETRIE COLLECTION.

Sentinel Duty (ca 1892), Charles M. Russell.
COURTESY OF RICHARD H. BISHOFF.

"Aw, come on, Kid," Jake coaxed, "he's known me all these months."

"Nope, can't help it," said Charlie.

"All right." Then Jake left for the cabin and returned with his Winchester. He climbed the hill back of the corral. It was a full half hour before that pig turned and faced Jake's way. Bang! The pet pig dropped.

After Jake had put his rifle away, he came over to Charlie. "He never knew what hit him. I don't think he saw me or knew who did it, do you? I had to bushwhack him."

Once while Jake was away on a trip to Fort Benton, Charlie stayed at the

Meat's Not Meat 'Till It's in the Pan (1915), Charles M. Russell.
GILCREASE MUSEUM, TULSA, OKLAHOMA (137.2244).

cabin to take care of the stock. Jake was getting quite civilized; he had a cow and some chickens. Though Charlie never could milk, Jake insisted he should do it while he was away.

Charlie remembered his early boyhood efforts and thought maybe he could do better now.

He began to milk. But he must have pinched the cow, for she kicked him half way across the corral. With the empty pail he returned to the cabin.

"It's no use—she kicks me out."

"Oh, that can't be," said Jake. "She's gentle."

"Do you think so? Well, how d'you s'pose I got these cow tracks all over my shirt front?"

Jake took the pail. "Come on, I'll show you how."

But it seemed that Mrs. Cow had just discovered how skilful she was, for she kicked Jake harder than she had Charlie.

Jake jumped up from the dust of the corral, hollering to Charlie to get the Winchester "so we can have some beef."

Charlie talked him out of that by persuading him that the milk belonged to the calf anyway.

Charlie—lonely during Jake's absence—hunted up the live stock for company. There was one game rooster that was boss among the young shanghais. If any of them crowed, Mr. Game ran him out in the brush. One day the game rooster crowed, and Charlie answered him. He crowed again; Charlie answered him.

When the rooster located the sound coming from Charlie, he took after him and Charlie ran. This kept up for about a week. Finally when Charlie appeared at the stable, the rooster came at him without crowing. Charlie would run, sometimes even letting the rooster spur him in the leg. Riding boots protected his legs and rooster thought he was boss.

The morning after Jake's return, he walked out into the corral wearing gumboots cut off for slippers. And the rooster came for him! He struck so hard that his spurs drew blood on Jake's leg. Jake grabbed a stick and broke the rooster's neck with a quick blow.

Charlie said, "Now that's a fine idea—killing an eight dollar rooster!"

"I don't care," Jake retorted. "Do you think I'm going to be run off the place by a chicken?"

Babcock and His Friends

[Charlie's friend] Old Bab was a man as rough as the mountains he loved, but he was all heart from the belt up. Friends and strangers were always welcome to shove their feet under his table. He was a great story-teller and could scare, entertain, and educate his audience with many a yarn.

Charlie used to give us this sample of Bab's yarns [aka "windies"]:

"I remember one night at his place in Pigeye Basin, Old Bab told about getting jumped by fifty hostile Sioux, a party that's been giving him a purty close run. The bullets and arrows is tearing up the dirt all around him when he hits the mouth of a deep canyon. He thinks he' safe, but riding up a ways, he finds it's a box canyon with walls from six hundred to one thousand feet straight up. His only chance to get away is back the way he came in, and the Indians are already whipping their ponies in there to the mouth of the canyon.

"Right at this point in the story, Old Bab rears back in his chair, closes his eyes and starts fondling his whiskers. This seems to be the end of the story, so one of his listeners speaks up:

"Well, what happened then, Bab?"

"Old Bab, with eyes still closed, takes a fresh chew [of tobacco] and whispers: 'They killed me.'"

Bab's place served as a sort of relay post-office for the miners and others living on the upper Judith, and Charlie received his mail there. On a trip with Bab down into the Basin, Charlie told him that he was expecting a letter from home.

Some days later when the little parcel of mail had arrived (it contained an inquiry for Charlie), Bab called him to one side. In a tone that was foreboding, he asked, "Kid, what you been doing down to Utica?"

"Why nothing, Bab. What's wrong?"

"Well," continued the old rancher, "I just got a letter from the sheriff, and things look pretty bad for you. Now, I tell you, Kid, I ain't for turning you in, but if that man-hunter shows up and you're here, I'm helpless. I'll tell you what you do—if you see anybody riding up in this direction, why you make for the hills and stay till they go."

Telling Some Windies (ca 1882-83), Charles M. Russell.
PETRIE COLLECTION.

Telling Some Windies depicts Charlie standing in Babcock's cabin listening to tall tales by the seated and seasoned mountain men. The full flavor of these occasions is well captured both in the powerfully moving rhetoric of Russell's illustrated letter celebrating the seventieth birthday of Brother Van Orsdel (see pages 43–45), as well as in Nancy's initial account here of Bab "fooling" or "joshing" his audiences.

Nothing out of the ordinary happened until late that afternoon when Charlie saw horsemen headed their way. He saddled Monty and struck out for the hills. He pulled up in the shelter of a coulee, from which point he could watch the ranch house.

He saw the riders tie their horses to the hitch-rack. Charlie dropped Monty's reins and sat watching developments. The visitors stayed until evening, then mounted their horses to ride back down the Judith hill.

It was dark and cold wind was blowing when Charlie showed up at the corral.

Old Bab had been waiting for him. "I had a hard time keeping them off of you, Kid, but I've got it fixed there. Everything's all right now," he said and handed Charlie a couple of letters.

It was at Old Bab's place, too, that Charlie first met the Reverend W.W. Van Orsdell (commonly known among Montanans as "Brother Van").

The following letter written years later [in 1918] to Brother Van gives Charlie's description of the people who visited at Bab's ranch:

"Dear Brother Van:

I received an invitation to your birthday party and more than sorry that I can't be there, but I am on the Jury." (Charlie despised serving on the jury, and since in Montana at that time one had to be a property owner to serve, Charlie had all his property transferred to my name.)

"I think it was about this time of year thirty-seven years ago that we first met at Babcock's ranch in Pigeye Basin on the Upper Judith. I was living at that time with a hunter and trapper, Jake Hoover, who you will remember. He and I had come down from the south fork with three pack horses loaded with deer and elk with old Bab, a man whose all-welcome way to strangers made the camp a hang-out for many homeless mountain and prairie men, and his log walls and dirt roof seemed like a palace to those who lived mostly under the sky.

"The evening you came, there was a mixture of bull whackers, hunters and prospectors, who welcomed you with hand shakes and rough but friendly greetings.

"I was the only stranger to you so after Bab introduced Kid Russell, he took me to one side and whispered, 'Boy,' says he, 'I don't savvy many psalm-singers but Brother Van deals square,' and when we all sat down to our elk meat, beans, coffee and dried apples, under the rays of a bacon grease light, these men who knew little of law and one among them, I knew wore notches on his gun, men who had

THE FOLLOWING LETTER WRITTEN YEARS LATER [IN 1918]
TO BROTHER VAN GIVES CHARLIE'S DESCRIPTION
OF THE PEOPLE WHO VISITED AT BAB'S RANCH

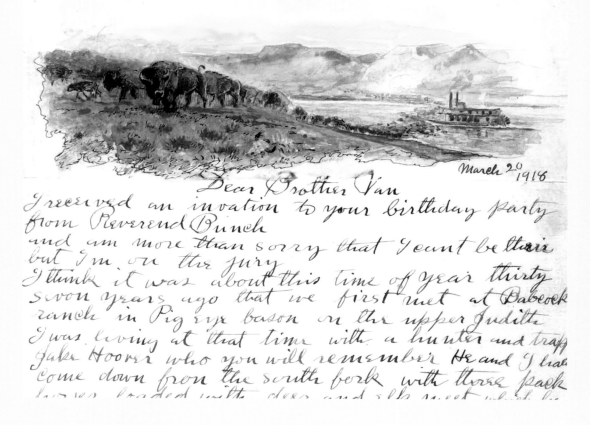

March 20 1918

Dear Brother Van

*I received an invation to your birthday party
from Reverend Bunch
and am more than sorry that I cant be there
but I'm on the jury
I think it was about this time of year thirty
seven years ago that we first met at Babcock
ranch in Pig eye bason on the upper Judith
I was living at that time with a hunter and trapper
Jake Hoover who you will remember He and I had
Come down from the south fork with three pack
horses loaded with deer and elk meat which he*

Letter to W.W. Van Orsdel (Brother Van), March 20, 1918, Charles M. Russell.
PETRIE COLLECTION.

On July 1, 1863, as some 93,000 Union troops met 70,000 Confederates at Gettysburg, Pennsylvania, Brother Van was a teenage boy carrying water to soldiers on the now legendary battlefield. Having personally witnessed the horrendous human carnage involving over 50,000 casualties at this turning point in the Civil War, Charlie's special friend of a later period, Brother Van Orsdel, underwent a religious epiphany. On the *Far West* paddle wheeler heading up the Missouri, he met both Sitting Bull and Buffalo Bill. After seminary and about to turn twenty-five years old he traveled west. He became an itinerant Methodist minister intent on addressing Montana's great need for such service, traversing on horseback throughout the state.

not prayed since they knelt at their Mother's knee, bowed their heads while you, Brother Van, gave thanks, and when you finished, someone said 'Amen.' I am not sure, but I think it was a man who I heard later was or had been a road agent.

"I was sixteen years old then, Brother Van, but have never forgotten your stay at old Bab's, with men whose talk was generally emphasized with fancy profanity, but while you were with us, although they had to talk slow and careful, there was never a slip. The outlaw at Bab's was a sinner and none of us there were saints, but our hearts were clean at least while you gave thanks when the Hold-up said 'amen.' You brought to the minds of those hardened, homeless men the faces of their mothers and few can be bad while she is near.

"I have met you many times since that, Brother Van, sometimes in lonely places but you never were lonesome or alone for a man with scarred hands and feet stood beside you and near Him there is no hate, so all you met loved you. 'Be good and you'll be happy' is an old saying which many contradict and say that 'goodness is a rough trail over dangerous passes with windfalls and swift deep rivers to cross.'

When the Land Belonged to God (1914), Charles M. Russell.
MONTANA HISTORICAL SOCIETY COLLECTION, HELENA, MONTANA (X1977.01.01).

Viewing the watercolor image on the top of the Brother Van letter on page 44, it is likely not coincidental that Charlie has placed an image closely resembling that of his 1914 masterpiece, *When the Land Belonged to God*.

"I have never ridden it very far myself but judging from the looks of you, it's a cinch bet that with a hoss called 'Faithe' under you, it's a smooth, flower grown trail with easy fords where birds sing and cold, clear streams dance in the sunlight all the way the pass that crosses the Big Divide. Brother Van, you have ridden that rail a long time and I hope you still ride to many birthdays on this side of the big range."

"With best wishes from my best half and me,
Your friend,
C.M. Russell."

[Nancy writes] In 1899 Brother Van was attending a Methodist conference in Great Falls. During this time he was a guest at our house. One morning as he sat watching Charlie paint, they were talking religion. Charlie said, "Brother Van, why are there so many different churches? It seems to me they would make a round-up and get it into one big church."

Brother Van smiled and said, "Yes, Charlie—the Methodist."

When Brother Van had graduated from the Seminary, he sang [songs] to pay his way up the Missouri River on the steamboat and started his missionary work, riding miles [on] horseback over those long trails between settlements. Sometimes he would find a bull whacker with his wagon mired down in mud, probably cursing a blue streak as he tried to get his wagon out. Brother Van would get off his horse, get right in and try to help the unfortunate bull whacker who cussed heartily while Brother Van said, "Praise the Lord!" The average plainsman respected this man of God and liked to hear him sing his favorite hymn, "Where is my wandering boy tonight?"

The friendship between Charlie and Brother Van lasted until the death of the latter in 1919.

A Taste of the Cow Business

IN THE SPRING OF 1881, Charlie's father sent him money to come home. To acknowledge it Charlie wrote a letter in which he said, "Thanks for the money, but I'm sending it back. I can't use it, but some day I'll make enough so I can come home to see you folks."

By the Spring of 1882 he had saved enough to return to St. Louis, where he stayed about four weeks. The city was too much for him. He had never liked crowds, and he could not resist the call back to Montana.

On his return trip he was to change trains in Kansas City, where he would have to wait for a north-bound train. The man who called the trains mumbled so that nobody could understand a word he said. An old Irishman [named Pat], also waiting for the train for the North, came to Charlie and asked, "Son, what's the man sayin'?"

Charlie answered, "I dunno."

"Now let's the both of us listen 'n see if we can understand 'im."

They could make nothing of the lingo. The Irishman said, "Come on, me son, let's the pair of us go up to 'im like gintlemen 'n ask 'im when our train goes."

[But the train conductor replied,] "I ain't here to answer questions but to call these trains, and when it's time, I'll do it—see?"

"Well, you gotta call 'em in a different language so as a man can understand ye!" [they both said]

After a time they thought they heard their train called and got aboard. When the conductor took up the tickets, he asked, "Where you going?"

Charlie answered, "To Butte, Montana."

"Well, not on this train," the conductor told them. "This goes to Texas!"

They had to get off in a small town to wait until 1 o'clock the next morning for their train. Soon after nightfall, all the lights in the town went out.

A farmer entered the depot where Charlie was trying to keep warm by the stove. Charlie looked up in his usual friendly fashion to say, "This is a nice country."

The farmer only looked at him and replied hesitantly, "Yes," and went to

When I Was a Kid (1905), Charles M. Russell.
C.M. Russell Museum, Great Falls, Montana, gift of Frederic G. and Ginger K. Renner,
IN MEMORY OF GRAHAM D. RENNER (2011.8.2).

Charlie Russell as a boy in St. Louis had dreamed of the far West and imagined him-self riding with the mountain men of olden times (*scene in the rocky mountains*, page 2); in 1905, he could look back on his two years with Jake Hoover in the Little Belt Mountains above the Utica Basin as a dream fulfilled. He had actually lived the life he had fantasized about "when I was a kid."

the other side of the stove. Charlie followed him around to remark, "You're having a fine winter."

"Yes," said the farmer, going to the other side of the stove again.

They played this ring-around-the-rosy business until Charlie gave up trying to talk. In a short time the farmer went outside. Charlie was sure the man was suspicious of him and fearing that he would be robbed, had gone out to "cache" his watch and all the decorations that hung on him! Upon his return he looked as though he had been trimmed.

Charlie and his Irish friend were glad to hear the noise of the approaching train which would take them to Butte. Since travelling was something of a luxury to them, they were going second class, which on that train was none too good.

But Charlie's partner asked the conductor what class they were travelling and was told "second class."

Exclaimed the Irishman, "In Heaven's name, what would third class be, a cattle car?"

The air in their coach was heavy with many kinds of odors, and in the morning they looked the train over with the hope of finding a change. The car was loaded with all kinds of people going West.

A German passenger held their attention. He gazed blankly ahead, with never a change of expression. He sat facing Charlie and the Irishman. Pat thought the German was looking at him and said to Charlie in a disguised tone, "What's the German lookin' at? He's got me nervous," and Pat looked out the window to get away from the blank-faced stare of their fellow passenger. In a few moments the Irishman asked Charlie, "is he lookin' at me yit?"

"No, but he's opening his lunch. We better get out."

There was also a Chinaman in the car who Charlie and his Irish friend decided was the only gentleman there.

They started forward to the smoker. They opened the door of the next car but closed it just as quickly, for the air was worse than that which they were just leaving. The Irishman asked Charlie in a hushed voice, "Are ye a good swimmer?" Kin ye hold yer breath long enough to go through, or shall we be after goin' over the top of the car to the smoker?"

When at last the train stopped at a station, Charlie and his new friend got out to walk in the welcome fresh air. They discovered that they were in

"WHY," SAID ED, "IT'S THE KID THAT DREW S.S. HOBSON'S RANCH SO REAL."

The Christmas Dinner (1898), pen and ink by Charles M. Russell; watercolor added by unknown individual.
COURTESY OF A PRIVATE COLLECTION.

This is a portrayal of two Indians asking for food at Christmas time. Ginger Renner indicates that the cabin is actually that of Jake Hoover, who is out front. His neighbor, S.S. Hobson, is in the doorway. Charlie is the standing figure to the left of Hoover.

a college town. A group of boys stood about to greet the new students as they stepped off the train. At the sound of their yells the Irishman exclaimed to Charlie, "Isn't it too bad! They're so young, too! I s'pose them buildings over there is the asylum."

Charlie arrived at Billings with a quarter in his pocket and two hundred miles between himself and [Jake] Hoover. Things looked "might rocky." He found an acquaintance from whom he borrowed a horse and saddle until he could get to his own in the Judith Basin country.

As it was early in April [1882], there was still a little snow. But after riding about fifteen miles, Charlie struck a cow outfit coming in to receive a thousand dogies for the Twelve Z and V outfit up the Basin. The boss, John Cabler, hired him [on the spot] to night-wrangle horses.

They were a month on the trail and turned loose at Ross Fork, where they were met by the Judith roundup. Charlie was getting back to Hoover and the country he knew, but he'd had a real taste of the cow business. He loved the life in the open country—no fences, just God and man in Nature's paradise.

To Horace Brewster, who had just fired his night herder, Cabler gave Charlie a good recommendation. He took the herd. It was a lucky thing no one knew him, he [Charlie] said later, or he would never have got the job.

Later, Old True asked who he was. Ed Older replied, "I think it's Kid Russell."

"Who's Kid Russell."

"Why," said Ed, "it's the kid that drew S.S. Hobson's ranch so real."

"Well," was True's reply, "if that's the Buckskin Kid, I'm bettin' we'll be afoot in the morning."

But after three or four days, Horace said, "That kid's going to be all right. He may hold them a little close on a dark night, but I'd a lot rather ride a hungry horse than be hunting them in the morning."

From that time on, Charlie was spoken of as "Kid Russell" and was liked by cow men. He held their bunch, which at that time numbered about four hundred saddle horses. That same fall Old True hired him to night herd beef, and for the most part of eleven years Charlie sang to their horses and cattle.

Night Watch (1922), Frank Tenney Johnson.
PETRIE COLLECTION.

In *Night Watch* by Frank Tenney Johnson, the artist, in effect, presents an homage to C.M. Russell, for whom Johnson had enormous respect. It portrays a night wrangler (referencing Charlie's main role in his eleven-year career as a cowboy). Here the rider is performing his key function of settling the white-faced cattle herd (in the lower right of the painting) by singing to them.

Only shortly before Russell's death, Los Angeles art dealer C.O. Middleton visited the artist and requested that Charlie sign a copy of *Rawhide Rawlins Stories*, which Middleton then also inscribed and gave to Frank and Vinnie Johnson (see page 176). The painting effectively captures Russell's fall cattle herd wrangling job complete with starlight and the lit cigarette.

Cows

CHARLIE NIGHT-HERDED HORSES in the Spring and beef in the Fall and became one of the most trusted horse wranglers and nightherders of beef in the Judith country. To be a successful nightherder of beef was to have attained a very responsible position on the range. The beef [and horses] represented the money of an outfit, and to have charge of this during the treacherous hours of summer and fall nights was to be entrusted with the capital and profits of the owners.

Startled by a sudden thunder storm on a dark night, or by the striking of a match by some careless cowpuncher, or by the mischievous cracking of an Indian blanket, a herd would often stampede and become transformed into the most unwieldy mass imaginable. Such an incident could result not only in loss of cattle but loss of human life. With a herd stampeding, and with the plains out into myriad forms by cutbanks and coulees, the herder endeavoring to head off the seething mass of hoof, horn and hide, never knew but that the next jump of his horse might mark his last moment on earth.

Charlie wrangled and nightherded for eleven years, and he never lost a herd.

He never did take kindly to bronchos, as their minds and his didn't seem to work together. It takes a special kind of man to ride a bad horse. He worked as a [daytime] cowpuncher only part of one season. That was in '83 on the Shonkin range. He admitted that he was sort of shaky at first, with so many horses [and cattle] in his care, but knew if he wanted to stick with the roundup and be a cowhand, he'd have to make a good showing right where he was—so he stuck [mostly to night wrangling].

[Teddy Roosevelt provides a real-life account of a personal experience involving a nocturnal stampede of cattle in the same era as when Charlie worked in the adjacent Montana territory to North Dakota:

"For a minute or two I could make out nothing except the dark forms of the beasts running on every side of me, and I should have been very sorry if my horse had stumbled, for those behind would have trodden me down. Then the herd split, part going to one side, while the other part seemingly

Musselshell Roundup (1919), Charles M. Russell.
PETRIE COLLECTION.

Charlie's experiences as a cowpuncher in 1883 were on the Musselshell Roundup in the southern part of the Judith Basin. This painting was executed in 1919 and represents Charlie's recollection of his romanticized youthful cowboying days.

In Bill Foxley's groundbreaking book, *Frontier Spirit*, the following observation is telling: *"Russell would have had a difficult time painting the exciting pictures we know him for had he been limited to present-day ranch life for his subjects. Today's Herefords, Angus and all the crosses have been scientifically bred for short, compact conformation and a placid disposition conducive to rapid weight gains. The cows Charlie knew in the 1880's were rangy, rawboned and wild and it took skill and a good deal of courage to handle them. Russell's admiration for the old time cowboy led to many of the dramatic, tension-packed paintings for which he is so well known. As the night wrangler for the DHS brand (Davis, Hauser, Stuart), Charlie worked the Musselshell round-up in 1883-84 and this painting is considered one of his great ones. There is no doubt that his all-seeing eye recorded the high rugged escarpments rising above the rolling hills, marked by scrubby Juniper and sage. The cowboys depicted in the painting were, no doubt, friends and working companions, their place in history marked by Charlie's recollections."*

kept straight ahead, and I galloped as hard as ever beside them. I was trying to reach the point—the leading animals—in order to turn them, when suddenly there was a tremendous splashing in front. I could dimly make out that the cattle immediately ahead and to one side of me were disappearing, and the next moment the horse and I went off a cut bank into the Little Missouri [River]. I bent away back in the saddle, and though the horse almost went down he just recovered himself, and, plunging and struggling through water and quicksand, we made the other side. . . . I galloped hard through a bottom covered with big cottonwood trees, and stopped the part of the herd that I was with, but very soon they broke on me again, and repeated this twice. Finally toward morning the few I had left came to a halt."

David McCullough observes in his book *Mornings on Horseback*, "By the time he finished that 'days work' he (Roosevelt) had been in the saddle nearly forty hours and worn out five horses." Roosevelt concludes in a letter to Henry Cabot Lodge, "I can now do cowboy work pretty well."]

Stampede at Night (ca 1888-89), Charles M. Russell.
Sketch sent with Charles M. Russell letter to William W. "Pony Bill" Davis, May 14, 1889.
PHOTOGRAPH COURTESY BRIAN W. DIPPIE COLLECTION, VICTORIA, BC.

THE PIEGANS CLAIMED AS THEIRS THE COUNTRY
FROM THE YELLOWSTONE IN THE SOUTH TO
THE BIG BOW (RIVER) IN THE NORTH.

Piegans (1908), Charles M. Russell.
REES-JONES COLLECTION, DALLAS, TEXAS.

Indians

THE INDIANS WEREN'T ANY TOO PLEASED at the start the cow business was getting [in Montana]. The Piegans claimed as theirs the country from the Yellowstone in the south to the Big Bow [River] in the north.

The Ross Fork camp was right on the Piegan trail to the Crow country, and there were many horse-stealing trips. [As a result] Every out-of-the-ordinary movement bothered Charlie.

One night Charlie had a bunch-quitter* necked to a steady horse. Along about midnight he was sure he saw a man on foot at the head of one of the horses. Slowly and cautiously he went around them, and he felt very foolish when he found that the 'man' was just the necked horse standing head-on so that he looked like a tall man.

On another afternoon Charlie was riding alone toward camp, enjoying the quiet and bigness of the country. Suddenly down the slope rode a band of Crows who had been following him for some distance. They started to shoot into the air, yelling as they began to ride in a circle, gradually closing in on him.

The Chief, wheeling rode straight at him.

"How!" said the Chief.

"How!" said Charlie.

The chief must have seen Charlie shaking and heard his teeth chattering, for the Indian said in broken English, "White boy much afraid?"

"I sure am!"

Then the chief said, "Not hurt you. Piegans steal Crow horses. Crows catch Piegans, make um cry like squaw. Now white boy go on to his people and stay close to their wagons. Piegans have bad hearts."

About four weeks later Charlie experienced his first [personal] adventure with the Piegans. He was alone in camp when two bucks appeared, wrapped to their eyes in their robes.

---

* bunch-quitter: an animal that will not stay with the herd. With horses, the bunch-quitter would be tied to the neck of a more reliable horse to keep him from leaving the herd.

THE MOON WAS SHINING.

The Horse Thieves (1901), Charles M. Russell.
PETRIE COLLECTION.

The shadowy landscape just left of the lead Indian appears to be the Judith Basin's Round Butte, placing this scene in the heart of the country where Charlie night wrangled.

Nancy's reference in her text to the shining moon and Charlie's artistic perspective as an undetected observer of the passing Indians along with the earlier statement about Ross Fork being on the horse-stealing trail to Crow Country strongly suggests that this incident could be the basis for Russell's exceptional nocturne oil painting, *The Horse Thieves*. About that painting, Russell scholar and historian Fred Renner tells us the legendary Piegan chief White Quiver is leading some fifty horses stolen from the Crow Indians through the Judith Basin toward the Blackfeet Reservation near Browning, Montana. Over the years, Charlie produced more than a half dozen variations of depictions of returning horse thieves, which underscores the deep impact of this experience for Russell.

Frederic Renner has asserted that the pinto with the prominent blaze on his forehead following White Quiver is the horse for whom Charlie traded his mare, as described on page 35. Monty's full story is captured in Russell's story "The Ghost Horse," originally published in 1919 and reprinted as a chapter in Russell's *Trails Plowed Under*.

One of them in a low yet commanding voice asked, "White boy cook?"

Charlie replies, "n-n-no, I can't cook."

The robe slipped from the shoulders of the warrior, who held in his arm a sawed-off gun. The Indian repeated his question, "You cook?"

"Y-y-yes, I can cook," and Charlie cooked until the visitors could hold no more.

Then the spokesman said, "White boy good cook," and added in a low-voiced, teasing manner, "You afraid?"

Another night that fall [of 1883], when Charlie was herding beef for True, he heard Indians singing. In a little while a small band of reds [Indians] rode out of a coulee about two or three hundred yards from him. The moon was shining. In its light Charlie could see them plainly. But they couldn't see him, as he'd slipped down beside his horse. They quit singing and stopped their horses when they saw the cattle. Charley kept quiet, and they went on.

Scouting Party (1900), Charles M. Russell.
PRIVATE COLLECTION, WYOMING.

Scouting Party shows a band of five braves led by the Piegan chief White Quiver, who was best known for his cleverly successful forays south to steal horses from the Crow Indians. This particular incident cited in Nancy's manuscript may actually have inspired Charlie's 1900 rendition of *Scouting Party*.

Charlie's Outfit

CHARLIE LIKED A GOOD RIG on his horse. He himself wore a good hat and boots. The rest of his clothes did not make so much difference to him. [However,] He was most careful of his outfit. His ropes were always neatly coiled, silver conchos polished, leather clean.

These trappings were a constant reminder of the people, their lives, and the country he was painting.

He could tell instantly how much a man knew about a rope if he threw it out straight, hondo end first. The minute an amateur took hold of it, he would tip his hand.

There were fashion leaders even among the cow people. These fellows put in a lot of time looking at their shadows cast by the sun as they rode along. In cloudy weather they were never very happy. And when a girl appeared in the neighborhood, these dandies found some excuse to show off for the lady!

Cowboy #2 (n.d.), Charles M. Russell, as reproduced in the Western Types print portfolio first published by the *Great Falls Daily Leader*. PETRIE COLLECTION.

Pea's Bottom
(Better Known as Poverty Flat)
1886

THIS WAS A LITTLE FARMING DISTRICT of about a thousand acres, laid out in the Yellowstone Valley. In this flat lived a dozen farmers. There were five women—four girls and a widow woman—the only white women within a hundred miles.

Once a year Con (Price) and Charlie used to work down into that country with the round-up. On the one night they were in that country, a big dance was always held.

The cook was musician; he played a mouthharp and a banjo at the same time, having an apparatus that held the harp to his mouth.

As in all communities, one girl was the belle—Molly Lane. All the cowpunchers in the outfit sought her favor, but the regular horse-wranglers and common cowboys never thought they had much chance and stepped back to give the wagon boss first chance, because he was, in dress and station, a bit higher on the social ladder. He usually monopolized most of Molly's time.

At one of these dances a waltz was played—ladies' choice, Charlie and Con, sure that they had little or no chance of being chosen by the belle, had retired to the kitchen of the two-room house to give more space to the dancers.

Con took a chew of tobacco in order to quiet his nerves while the dance was going on. Just as his chew got nice and juicy, along came Miss Molly to ask him for a dance! Rather than let her know he would do such a thing as chew tobacco, he swallowed the whole mouthful.

They went through the dance. Ordinarily Con would have been very sick, but this time he wasn't affected, because he was too excited at being given a chance to dance with Molly. Charlie, spellbound in admiration of Con, stood still and watched them dance. [Con confirms all the elements of this story in his second autobiography, *Trails I Rode* (Pasadena, CA: Trails' End Publishing Co., 1947), pp. 79–81.]

THOUGH HE HIMSELF NEVER PLAYED,
HE WAS INTERESTED IN THE SIGHT
OF TWO MEN PLAYING FOR BIG STAKES.

Faro Layout (ca 1910) Charles M. Russell,
AS PUBLISHED IN *THE VIRGINIAN* BY OWEN WISTER (NEW ILLUSTRATED EDITION, 1911).

This pen and ink drawing of a faro game was done by Charlie as an illustration of a scene in the classic western novel, *The Virginian*, by Owen Wister. As Nancy's account confirms, while Russell did not personally play the game, he was quite intrigued to watch it played for high stakes in the western wilds of Montana.

Glimpses of Life

IN THE WINTER OF '86 Charlie was watching a big-limit game called Farobank. Though he himself never played, he was interested in the sight of two men playing for big stakes.

They were losing. One had already lost five or six hundred dollars and was making a most awful howl about it, walking the floor, kicking his chair over, breaking chips and swearing. He thought his luck might change after this outbreak, so he sat down again.

But there was a fellow standing behind him—and to a gambler, this is always a hoodoo. He looked around to see the most peculiar pair of hands resting on the back on his chair. They were enormous. He started counting the fingers. There were five instead of four beside the thumb!

He gasped and looked again, saying, "I've heard o' the big mitt, but I've never saw it before; who in the hell could have luck with that behind him?" and he pointed backward at the strange creature behind him. "That's as bad as a cross-eyed man watchin' you play!"

Turning to the other loser, he stormed "Why don't you say somethin'? What kind of a man are you, sittin' thar like you're froze? [You have] Lost five or six times as much as I have and ain't said nothin'!"

The other fellow pulled his hand out of his shirt front, where it had been tucked, opened his shirt to show blood blisters on the skin where he had pinched himself to keep from saying anything.

"I ain't said nothin', but it hurts jest the same and I'm quittin'."

OH Ranch Wagon in Mud (ca 1896), Charles M. Russell.
PETRIE COLLECTION.

The depiction of cowboys moving the OH Ranch wagon uphill through the mud involved an incident that Charlie had probably personally experienced in the fall of 1886. The posture of the figure on the left bears a striking resemblance to others known to be of young Charlie. For example, see the similar posture of the figure and angle of the hat on the right side of the image below, *Kickover of Morning Coffee Pot*. The action on the OH Ranch was all occurring in the fall of 1886 leading up to the disastrous winter for cattle ranching of 1886–1887, known as "The Great Die Up" among Montana cattlemen.

Kickover of Morning Coffee Pot (ca 1896), Charles M. Russell.
PETRIE COLLECTION.

Waiting for a Chinook

This incident in Russell's career has been published the world over. The story as told and printed has, however, assumed many different forms, almost never twice alike. [To clarify Charlie's own recollections of the event, and knowing since his recent return from the Mayo Clinic that his remaining time was likely to be short, Judge James W. Bollinger, who visited the Russells at Lake McDonald each summer, arranged for this carefully recorded interview.] *The following was taken stenographically from the dictation of Mr. Russell himself at Lewis Glacier Hotel, Lake McDonald, Montana, now known as the Lake McDonald Lodge, on August 6, 1926.*

"THE WINTER OF '86 AND '87 all men will remember. It was the hardest winter the open range ever saw. An awful lot of cattle died. The cattle would go in the brush and hump up and die there. They were not rustlers. A horse will paw and get grass but a cow won't. Then the wolves fattened on the cattle.

"In the fall of '86 there was good grass. The country was all open—no fences. The horses got through the winter fat. They could paw through the snow. If I remember right, the snow didn't come until after Christmas— pretty late—had a pretty nice winter till then. When she did come, she stayed. There was two feet on the level. The stage line had to have men stick willows in the snow so they would know where the road was. Those willows in part of the road were [still] standing in May.

"Now, I was living at the "O H" Ranch that winter. There were several men there, and among them was Jesse Phelps, the owner of the "O H." One night Jesse Phelps had got a letter from Louis Kaufmann [Lewis E. Kaufman], one of the biggest cattle men in the country, who lived in Helena, and Louis wanted to know how the cattle were doing, and Jesse says to me, "I must write a letter to Louie and tell him how tough it is."

"I was sitting at the table with him, and I said, "I'll make a sketch to go with it." So I made one, a small water color about the size of a postal card, and I said to Jesse, "Put that in your letter." He looked at it and said, "Hell, he don't need a letter; that will be enough."

THE COW IN THE PICTURE IS A 'BAR R' COW—
ONE OF KAUFMANN'S BRANDS.

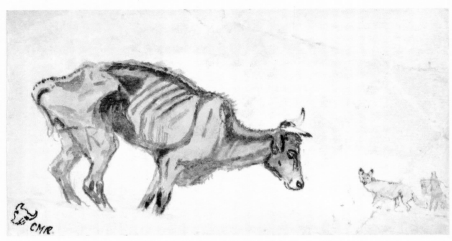

Waiting for a Chinook (The Last of 5,000) (1887), Charles M. Russell.
Used with permission from the Montana Stockgrowers Association, Helena, Montana.
IMAGE COURTESY OF THE MONTANA HISTORICAL SOCIETY (L1953.01.01).

The "Bar R" cow brand is on right rear leg. The tiny original watercolor arrived in Helena in early April 1887, thus dating the picture. It created a minor sensation in the Montana press and cemented Russell's reputation as the "Cowboy Artist." In the first half of the twentieth century it was widely circulated as a postcard after Ben Roberts copyrighted it in 1907.

"The cow in the picture is a 'Bar R' cow—one of Kaufmann's brands. I wrote on the picture myself, 'Waiting for a Chinook,' and nothing else. There was no number of cattle, no 'Last of Five Thousand,'—just 'Waiting for a Chinook.'"

"When Kaufmann received it in Helena, he got drunk on the strength of the bad news and gave the picture to Ben Roberts, a saddler. And Ben kept it until a few years ago, then sold it to a cattle man on the Musselshell River, a Mr. Heidekoper, who still owns it. He lives a part of the time now on the Musselshell and part of the time in Billings. Had a big ranch there. Mr. Heidekoper told me when he got through with it that he would give it to the State Historical Society of Montana. [It actually is now owned by the Montana Stockgrowers and held in the custody of the Montana Historical Society.] I think Louie Kaufmann told me that he would have given this fellow four or five hundred dollars for it. He thought Ben Roberts sold it for about a hundred.

"Heidekoper brought the card to Great Falls and asked me if I would sign it and say that it was the original, and I did. It was already signed by Kaufmann, certifying that it was the original.

"That card has given me great publicity, especially among the cattle men in Montana who knew about that awful winter. But it was long years after that before I made any money painting pictures."

Cowboy in a Snow Storm (ca 1888-89), Charles M. Russell.
Sketch sent with Charles M. Russell letter
to William W. "Pony Bill" Davis, May 14, 1889.
PHOTOGRAPH COURTESY BRIAN W. DIPPIE COLLECTION, VICTORIA, BC.

THE ROUNDUP [CAMP] WAS [JUST OUTSIDE OF]
UTICA IN THE JUDITH BASIN.

Round Up Camp (ca 1889), Charles M. Russell.
PETRIE COLLECTION.

Charlie's roundup camp experiences, largely occurring in the mid to late 1880s, provided a wealth of material both for his artwork and his stories in *Rawhide Rawlins
Stories*, *More Rawhides*, and *Trails Plowed Under*.

1887

WHEN CHARLIE AND KAY LOWRY were working for the Judith Basin round-up, "reps" (representatives) were sent to get the cattle that used to drift off their home range. The "reps" went to an outside wagon and working with them all over their range, held what cattle they found, carrying them along with them until they got the home range worked. The "rep" was expected to know all the irons [i.e., brands] of the company he represented and to attend every round-up.

They sent Kay Lowry and Charlie as "reps" over there. Each round-up had a captain who was boss of the entire set-up. He laid out the work, and his word was law.

Spurgeon was captain of the Mocassin round-up where Charlie and Kay Lowry went to "rep." He was a great friend of Charlie's and joked with him a good deal.

With him Charlie had taken some of his little tubes of paint, and Kay Lowry had brought his violin. They packed them in their beds for the hundred-mile trip.

That autumn after the round-up, Charlie's and Kay's original boss who had sent them over there to "rep" met Jim Spurgeon in Lewistown and inquired why he had got only a few of the Basin cattle.

Spurgeon answered, "How would you expect to get cattle, sending an artist and a violinist over there to rep?"

Breakfast on the Judith Basin Roundup at Utica (ca 1886), Culver Studio.
C.M. RUSSELL MUSEUM, GREAT FALLS, MONTANA, GIFT OF PHIL AND KAREN KORELL (989.8.1).

This is the roundup crew that Nancy describes as dedicated to drinking Utica dry.
Charlie is in the front row, third from the left.

Plunkett's Run-away Train
(1887)

THE ROUNDUP [CAMP] was [just outside of] Utica in the Judith Basin. Frank Plunkett and the others were trying to make it a dry town by drinking it all up. But there was still plenty of liquor flowing, even when the fellows had had all they could carry.

Plunkett wanted a change from horseback riding. He hired a team and buggy, insisting on taking Charlie for a buggy ride. Plunkett had been drinking more than Charlie realized, and Charlie hadn't had enough to become callous to danger.

As he watched Plunkett's condition, he found himself getting more sober every minute. After they got out a way, Plunkett was going so fast that Charlie asked him to let him drive. But Plunkett knew Charlie didn't know anything about driving. Suspecting what was in his companion's mind, Plunkett cried out, "Hell! We'll both die together!" and threw the reins away.

Of course, the team upset their wagon and threw them out. They were able to walk back to town. By the time they arrived, both were sober enough to start drinking all over again, convinced that they were heroes.

Charlie did not like the new. He was a child of the open west

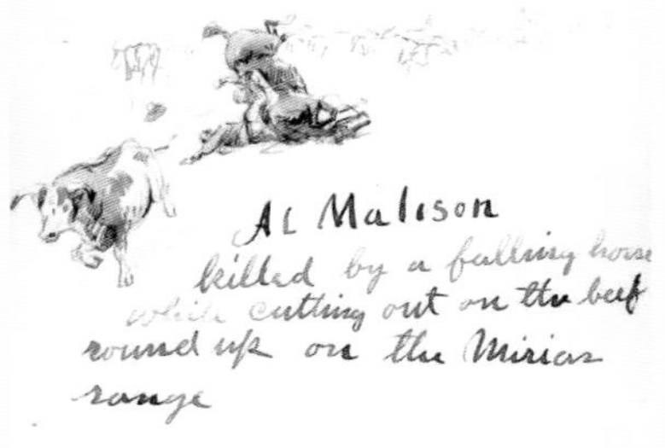

Al Malison
killed by a falling horse
while cutting out on the beef
round up on the Mirias
range

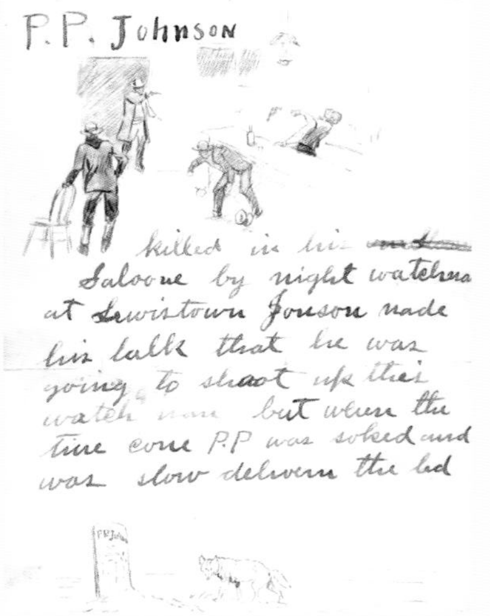

P.P. Johnson
killed in his ~~and~~
Saloone by night watchman
at Lewistown Jonson made
his talk that he was
going to shoot up this
watch man but when the
time come P.P was soked and
was slow delivern the led

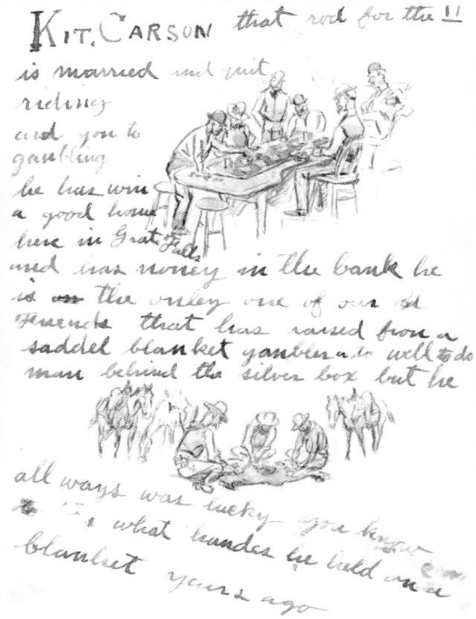

Kit Carson that rode for the 11
is married and quit
riding
and gone to
gambling
he has won
a good house
here in Grat Falls
and has money in the bank he
is the onley one of our old
friends that has raised from a
saddel blanket gambler to a well to do
man behind the silver box but he
all ways was lucky you know
what hands he held on a
blanket years ago

Letter to Harry T. "Tommie" Duckett, July 1901, Charles M. Russell.
PETRIE COLLECTION.

These are three of the pages from an eleven-page illustrated letter from Charlie Russell in July 1901, updating his longtime cowboy friend, Tommie Duckett (quoted on page 75), about happenings involving others they both knew. As these pages indicate, of the eleven people mentioned, Russell describes seven who died under various violent circumstances.

Cow Days
are Changing

CHARLIE WAS HERE TO WITNESS the changes, as can be seen by this excerpt from [an October 17, 1919] letter to Harry Stanford:

"When the 'Nester' turned this country grass side down, the West we loved died. She was a beautiful girl who had many lovers, but today there are only a few left to mourn her. If the few old lovers that still camp this side of the big range would write about her, she would not be forgotten. [Two years later, in 1921, Charlie published his first edition of *Rawhide Rawlins Stories* as his and Nancy's effort to ensure that "she" (the West) was not forgotten.]

I [Charlie] spent New Year's in Lewistown and met some of our old friends. Time has hung his work on them the same as me. You wouldn't know the town or the country either. It's all grass side down where once you rode circle and I night-wrangled. A gopher couldn't graze. I like[d] it better when it belonged to God. It was sure his country when we first knew it."

Charlie did not like the new. He was a child of the open West before wire or rail spanned it. Civilization choked him. Even in 1889 when the Judith Country was getting well settled and the sheep had the range, he resented the change and followed he cattle north to the Milk River, trying to stay in an open-range country.

[In a late 1880s letter to "Pony Bill" Davis] He [Charlie] said, "I expect I will have to ride to the end of my days, but I would rather be a poor cow puncher than a poor artist."

He didn't know that he was graduating from Nature's College and the teaching frontiersmen had given him. He was about ready to go back over the trails he had travelled to leave for the coming generation a record of the changes he had seen.

In the fall of 1891, he received a letter from Charlie Green, better known as "Pretty Charlie," who was in Great Falls. He wrote that if

SO CHARLIE SADDLED HIS GRAY
AND PACKED MONTY, THE PINTO

Charles Russell on Grey Eagle leading Monte (n.d.), photographer unknown.
GILCREASE MUSEUM, TULSA, OKLAHOMA (TU2009.39.5676A-B).

Charlie would come to that camp, he would make seventy-five dollars a month and grub.

It looked good, so Charlie saddled his gray and packed Monty, the pinto, and pulled his freight for said burg.

Upon his arrival he was introduced to Mr. K. who pulled out a contract as long as a stake rope for him to sign. But Charlie wouldn't sign until he had tried out the plan. Mr. K. gave him ten dollars on account, saying that he would see him later.

After a few days he met Charlie and wanted to know why he had not started to work. Charlie replied that he had had to find a place to live and to get his supplies.

The contract read that everything Charlie modelled or painted for a year was to be the property of Mr. K., who wanted him to paint from early morning to night. Charlie argued that there was some difference between painting and sawing wood. He balked. He hunted up a fellow from whom he could borrow ten dollars to repay Mr. K. Charlie said he could not work under pressure, so they split up and Charlie started out for himself.

He put in with a bunch of cow punchers, a round-up cook and a prize fighter out of work. They rented a shack on the south side of town. The "feed" was very short at times, but they wintered.

(The following is an excerpt from a letter written by Tommie Duckett). "In early days, white men were not numerous in Montana, and we all knew each other. If any man had any particular ability or characteristic, it was pretty generally known to all. That in a measure accounts for the fact that Charlie's ability to paint pictures was well known over the entire Northwest even in the early days. At that time, many of his pictures possessed undoubted artistic merit and gave a hint of his great future genius.

[Tommie Duckett continues] I would be derelict in my duty if I did not here make some mention of the sterling character of my friend which in those days of his early manhood and my own, stand forth so prominently. Charlie had a keen sense of humor that manifested itself always. He was fond of his friends and extremely tolerant of those who had forfeited his friendship. He never complained, and I do not remember him

THESE BUCKEROOS ARE MORE LIKE
THE COW PUNCHER OF LONG AGO THAN
ANY I'VE SEEN [RECENTLY].

A Cowboy (ca 1888-89), Charles M. Russell.
Sketch sent with Charles M. Russell letter to William W. "Pony Bill" Davis, May 14, 1889.
PHOTOGRAPH COURTESY BRIAN W. DIPPIE COLLECTION, VICTORIA, BC.

I USED TO THINK THE OLD TIME COW PUNCHERS WERE
PRETTY FANCY IN THE NORTH COUNTRY, BUT FOR PRETTY
THESE MEXICANS MAKE THEM LOOK LIKE DIGGERS.

Letter to Robert Stuart ("Friend Bob"), January 16, 1907, Charles M. Russell.
Ink, transparent and opaque watercolor, and graphite on paper;
Amon Carter Museum of American Art, Fort Worth, Texas,
AMON G. CARTER COLLECTION (1961.365.2).

showing any degree of ill temper. He was honest and honorable in all his dealings."

Next Spring Charlie went back to the Milk River country and once more the range life, but it had changed. In the fall of 1892 he returned to Great Falls, took up the paint brush and never rode the range again. But he never missed an opportunity of attending contests or rodeos—anything that brought back the old life with men and horses in action.

In 1906 Charlie [with Nancy and his father, Charles Silas Russell] visited Old Mexico to study the cow people down there.

"It's sure an old-time cow country," he wrote. "I travelled from the north line to within a few hundred miles of the isthmus and never saw a wire— it's all open range. I used to think the old time cow punchers were pretty fancy in the North country, but for pretty these Mexicans make them look like diggers. I was on the range of Torassia [Luis Terrazas], the biggest cow man in the world. It takes a thousand riders to work his country. He only branded 75,000 calves last Spring besides his cows. He owns thousands of horses and mules. The vaquero does not use a wagon. His grub and bedding is packed on mules and the mules ain't overloaded. Their bill of fare is beef, beans, corn meal and red pepper. That is, I think so from some of the feed I got.

"Where every man wears his own bed [i.e., the draped blanket of the figure on page 77], there is no use for a bed wagon. They were paid from eight to ten dollars a month with grub, but as muscal (their whiskey) is one cent a drink, they have a good time. One drink of this booze will make a jack rabbit spit in a rattle snake's eye, and as all Mexicans pack knives, cow outfits often leave town short-handed.

"God knows the booze we got was bad enough, but I believe if we had muscal at the Mexican price with our wage, every cow outfit would have needed a hearse instead of a bed wagon. As it is, it was bad enough. We both know many cow punchers that fell under the smoke of a 45 that are taking their long sleep in a hole on the prairie.

"The cattle in Mexico are all Spanish long horns and are sure wild."

———

[Years later Charlie further recounts:]

"In May 1926, I was at the Quien Sabe Ranch near Holliston, California. They branded out a thousand calves. These buckeroos are more like the cow puncher of long ago than any I've seen [recently]. They still use centerfire saddles and a rawhide rope. Most of them use rawhide reins and they are dally men. Maybe they can't work as fast as the tie men but they sure do their work pretty. California is the only place I ever saw real cow girls. There were a few on this ride that could handle a rope but they didn't look like they knew what a lipstick was. Their eyebrows were the ones God gave them, and it's a cinch bet they knew more about a brand book than the *Ladies Home Journal*.

———

[In a March 28, 1925, letter to Harry Stanford Charlie observed:]

"A few years ago a wise man said that a mountain goat had ticks that gave man the spotted fever. Mankind is all for himself. He wants to kill the mountain goat because he packs spotted fever. Where a goat lives, he might have chills, but it's a cinch he'd never get feverish. They've plowed out the grass and got tumble weed. Since the coyotes thinned out there is lots of gophers. Killing the prairie chicken and sage hen has made it good for grasshoppers. Now they say the horse eats grass and breeds flies. I've been back to kitchens a hundred miles from a horse and a horse couldn't have lived there for flies. Maybe when they kill off all the horses, the flies will come to town leaving this awful animal, that horse, that is a germ carrier. The flies will bring glanders to men—won't that be hell?"

"Folks will be glad to see the vet when he comes with his Winchester. I don't think they'd say all these things about a horse but [what] they [really] want [is] to sell his meat. I think a horse is the cleanest animal on earth, but I couldn't eat a friend. There are men I'd rather eat than some horses. I know if they'd kill men off as soon as they were useless, Montana wouldn't be so crowded. We wouldn't have so much law, no keys, and all the bootleggers would starve to death. Not that I have anything against a bootlegger— they're only trying to give folks what the law took away [i.e., prohibition of alcohol]. If I don't quit belly-achin', some law maker will put the useless irons on me. I'm sorry to hear they are killing range horses in Montana. I've got two on the Flathead Reservation and suppose when I want them I'll get them with a can opener."

The Cascade Studio

[Manuscript draft, Charles M. Russell Research Collection (Britzman),
Gilcrease Museum, Tulsa, OK, C.8.231]

THE ROBERTS'S [BEN ROBERTSES] had several small houses or shacks, as they were called. Charlie rented one of them and turned it into a make-shift studio—that is, he had a box for an easel, an old chair, and his roll of bedding in a tarpaulin. On the floor was his war bag with his personal effects. At another place on the floor, his saddle, chaps, and horse-jewelry.

He had just filled a number of orders for a wealthy St. Louisian [the Niedringhaus family was Russell's early supporter with art purchases], the work amounting to several hundred dollars. He had been painting in Great Falls for the past three years, after leaving the cow range and had sold his pictures as fast as he painted them.

Charlie was a sociable person, so he spent too much time with what he called "the bunch" and could not get down to work which was his reason for coming to Cascade where he immediately drew a crowd of punchers around him in his new home and they started batching. Charlie could usually make a grub stake and cowpunchers were not as a rule flush in the winter.

Contrast in Artist's Salons—Charlie Painting in His Cabin (ca 1894),
Charles M. Russell. Ink, transparent watercolor, and graphite on paper;
AMON CARTER MUSEUM OF AMERICAN ART, FORT WORTH, TEXAS, AMON G. CARTER COLLECTION (1961.305.1)

The Barber and the Blacksmith
1891

IN CASCADE THE BLACKSMITH BET the barber all his money—four dollars—that he could ride the first broncho that came to town.

The barber bet him that he couldn't.

They appointed Charlie stake-holder. Con Price happened to ride the first broncho into town. It was also the first time that bronc had been ridden.

The barber wanted to make sure that the horse would buck when the money was put up, and the blacksmith wanted to make equally sure that the horse wouldn't buck, so that he could win the money.

Con couldn't guarantee either one. Since Charlie was stake-holder and both he and Con wanted the eight dollars for joy juice, Con went to Charlie for advice.

Charlie told him to tell the blacksmith the horse wouldn't buck and to tell the barber just the opposite. Thus the bet was made. The blacksmith mounted the horse, one hand holding close to the horn. He was a big, strong man. He grasped the bridle rein, and [the] horse started off at a walk.

The blacksmith had ridden him about one hundred yards without a mishap, when a sheep man on his way home from town leaped up by the bronco and flapped his big overcoat in the bronc's face.

The bronco threw down his head. The saddle horn hit the blacksmith in the eye, and he was thrown off on the ground. With both hands over his black and swollen eye, he struggled up to his feet, saying, "I've lost the bet, boys! But if it hadn't been for that damn sheepherder, I'd a won!"

However, Charlie, the stakeholder, had the stakes, and they proceeded to enjoy them.

"Cascade" 1895
[Nancy and Charlie Meet]

[Manuscript draft, Charles M. Russell Research Collection (Britzman), Gilcrease Museum, Tulsa, OK, C.8.231]

TWENTY-FIVE MILES SOUTH of Great Falls, Montana, on the bank of the Missouri River, is the little town of Cascade. It has one of the loveliest surroundings you can imagine; to the east and north a broad valley cupped in by mountains, on the west a great butte rises up as if in protection of the settlement. The river flows north so that you can see away through for miles in that direction.

In one of the snug homes located near the river's bank, there was great excitement. A distinguished guest was expected—Charlie Russell, the cowboy artist was coming for a visit!

We, the children, three Roberts' children, Gorham, ten, Hebe six, Vivian two; and I, Nancy Cooper, seventeen, had heard of him and how much he knew about Indians and old cowboys and the Wild West. He could draw them showing us just how they looked and tell us how they lived!

Mrs. Roberts had told us she knew Mr. Russell in Helena, when he first came to Montana in 1880. Mrs. Roberts and I were getting the supper on the table when Gorham came bouncing in with "Oh, Mother, he's here!" Then, we heard voices, that of Mr. Roberts and the stranger. They were coming near the back door. There was a jingle of spur-rowels, on the steps, then a call "Leila, here's Charlie!" and Mrs. Roberts went to meet them.

They came in and we were introduced in that clean, spacious kitchen. The table was covered with a red and white cloth, a wood fire was burning in the cook stove, the biscuits were ready to be put into the oven, and supper was to be served in fifteen minutes.

Our cowboy guest took his Stetson off of a very erect, blonde head and said, "I'm glad to meet you", and shook hands with all of us, even the baby. Then, taking off his spurs, he said "I'd like to wash".

On a bench near the back door was a wash-pan, soap and a pail of water, hanging on the door a roller towel. He was told to help himself, while we put the supper on the table.

Charles M. Russell in front of Square Butte (n.d.), photographer unknown.
PETRIE COLLECTION.

Both Charlie and Nancy recognized the appeal of Montana landmarks such as Cascade's Square Butte in his paintings. This picture was probably "photoshopped" even before such a term was coined. It shows an older Charlie with Square Butte framed by his horse's underside and legs. One cannot help but wonder if this was Nancy's creative device for reminding her husband's market of his deep identification with old Montana. Or perhaps it was simply a sentimental reminder for her of their beginnings together in Cascade, when they were young and their humble pleasures shone golden in memory. The picture was found among items in the Nancy Russell estate.

There was something different about this man. He took off his coat, a double-breasted blue serge, hung it on a chair-back, turned very square shoulders and straight back to me and walked over to the wash-bench. He was very little above average height and weight. His high-heeled riding boots covered small arched feet, his riding breeches were snug-fitting of heavy blue army cloth. In fact, they were Northwest Mounted Police pants, I learned later. They were held up by a wonderful bright colored French half-breed sash that clung just above the hip bones. The sash was wound around twice, the ends twisted and turned into a queer flat knot, the long fringe tucked into his hip pocket and a gray flannel shirt unbuttoned at the throat with a neck tie hanging loosely. It was worn because a tie was supposed to be a part of the civilized man's dress—not that it was needed or wanted by him. His face, with its square jaw and chin, large mouth, tightly closed firm lips, the under protruding slightly beyond the short upper, straight nose, high cheek bones, gray-blue deep-set eyes that seemed to see everything but with an expression of honesty and understanding. In time I came to know that he could not see wrong in anybody. He never believed anyone did a bad act intentionally, it was always an accident.

His hands were good-sized, perfectly shaped with slender long fingers. He loved jewelry and always wore three or four rings. They would not have been Charlie's hands any other way. Everyone noticed his hands. [I]t was not the rings that attracted but the artistic, sensitive hands that had great strength and charm. When he talked he used them a lot to emphasize what he was saying, much as an Indian would do.

While he washed, I watched him as closely as possible without being observed. When he was drying his face, there seemed to be a chance to take a good look, from boots up. By the time my eyes reached his head, he was drying one side of his face and peeking out of one corner of the towel at me. He laughed and I almost dropped the plate of fried ham. "Are the potatoes burning and Nancy will you please get the quince preserves in the cellar way?" Mrs. Roberts saved me in my great confusion by asking me to do the things I knew I should do.

There must be a gun hidden away some where in that sash but it could not be seen though I tried my hardest because it was not there. This man was not a gun-man but a gentle, lover of Nature. We all learned this as the years passed.

At the supper table in the soft light of the coal oil lamp, he talked. We could see the play of laughing wrinkles on that Indian-like face. He looked like a blond Indian and had us fascinated with his stories of real life.

IN THE SILVERDOLLAR SALOON, HIS FRIENDS WERE JOKING
WITH HIM ABOUT HAVING A GIRL UP AT CASCADE.

Charlie Russell Proposes to Nancy Cooper (ca 1896), Charles M. Russell.
National Cowboy & Western Heritage Museum, Oklahoma City, Oklahoma.
GIFT OF JASPER D. ACKERMAN (1977.30).

In her original hand-corrected typescript draft of this biography, Nancy set up her story about Charlie's return to Cascade from a spree in Great Falls by writing: *"About two months after Charlie and I were engaged, he thought he should go to Great Falls to see a fellow."* Omitting any reference to their engagement deprives the story of its context. The spree was a celebration—in effect, a bachelor party for Charlie held at the Silver Dollar by his old Great Falls cronies. Responsibly, he had left his horses at home and taken the train.

His engagement to Nancy was a life-altering event, and in an endearing watercolor drawing he made at the time, a flustered Charlie pops the question on a moonlight stroll with that "girl up at Cascade."

———

About two months after Charlie and I met [in late 1895], he thought he should go to Great Falls to see a fellow. He did not go horse-back but on the train, leaving his two horses, Monty and Redbird, in the pasture, as he expected to be back in a few days.

In the Silverdollar saloon, his friends were joking with him about having a girl up at Cascade.

One evening Bill Rance [future owner of the Silver Dollar Saloon] telephoned Mr. Roberts that Charlie had been detained for a few days. Then he turned to say in a low, but perfectly audible, voice, "Don't try to come to the phone, Charlie. If you keep still, they won't know you're drunk." Then he explained to Mr. Roberts, "Oh, Mr. Russell can't come to the phone—he's very busy." Again in the low voice, "If you don't keep still, they'll know you're loaded and can't get to the phone!"

This was all a joke for my benefit, because Mr. Roberts had hardly finished telling us that Charlie would not be back for some time when in he walked with a friend, Jack Coats, who had returned on the train with him for a visit.

I noticed Charlie's husky voice and said anxiously, "Oh, you've taken cold!"

Coats smiled at his guilty partner, who said, "I guess I must have slept near an open window or in a draft."

The truth of the matter was that they had not slept and did not remember how they had got to Cascade. Charlie said he had a hazy recollection of sitting somewhere on the train with Coats opposite him. They had both been asleep when Charlie became conscious that something was wrong. He opened his eyes and looked down and thought, "Have I gone mad? Am I frothing at the mouth?"

There were little bunches of fluff or bubbles all over his coat. He felt his face. It was dry. He looked over at Coats, who was still asleep. But Coats stirred, half cleared his throat and spit straight out. The fuzzy stuff lit on Charlie, who said it was a great relief to know he wasn't doing it himself!

When Coats awakened in the shack at Cascade, he thought he was in a livery stable, so many ropes, bridles, saddles, blankets and pack-saddles were scattered about.

"Hey, son," he called out, "whose stable are we in?"

My Valentine (1896), Charles M. Russell.
MONTANA HISTORICAL SOCIETY COLLECTION, HELENA, MONTANA (X1954.03.03).

Peaceful Valley Saloon (ca 1896), Charles M. Russell, as reproduced as a limited run print.
PETRIE COLLECTION.

Peaceful Valley Saloon was painted by Charlie in 1896 as payment for the rental of his wedding suit. Michael Flinn has stated, *"When Charlie was to wed Nancy he needed a suit. My grandfather had a general store in Cascade, Montana, 'Sheppard and Flinn.' He loaned Charlie a suit for the wedding. As a thank you, Charlie painted this scene from the 'Cyote Kelly Peacful Vally Saloon.' In my youth, I frequented many similar establishments and it was not always peaceful."*

Cascade 1896
[The Wedding]

WHEN CHARLIE WROTE HOME that he was engaged to be married, he said, "Cupid has bushwhacked me—he shot me when I wasn't looking. Until now I haven't thought much about flowers, but this girl of mine loves them so much, I am falling for them, too."

Father's answer was, "Charlie, have you stopped to think what it will mean to you to earn a living for two? It is something to consider. You've been free to go where you pleased and when it pleased you; it didn't make any difference whether you had a place to sleep or not, as you carried your bed on a packhorse. Any place under the stars has been your home. It won't be that way after you take a wife."

When Charlie brought me that letter, his only comment was, "I got as good a chance as any of these Sunday School boys to be good to you."

We were married September 9, 1896. There were just nine people present at the very short ceremony which took place in the Roberts' living-room at eight o'clock in the evening. Charlie gave ten dollars to the preacher who tied the knot and five dollars to the fellows around town to keep them from chivareeing us.

After the refreshments (I made the wedding cake and Charlie had frozen the ice cream), Charlie and I started on our journey through life in what he called "double-harness."

He had spent seventy-five dollars—all he had—to fit up the shack that was to be our new home. It contained one room, 12 x 24 [feet], with a small lean-to kitchen at the back. The room was wainscoted. Charlie had made valiant attempts to paint it a light blue, but he was not very skillful with that kind of paint and brush, and he had had to give up the job to a half-breed Indian who did odd jobs around Cascade.

Charlie had a variety of Indian equipment with which we decorated the walls of our honeymoon house. These relics looked very nice on our walls.

We were short of chairs. But in one corner we had a willow back rest against its tripod, and we had flung over it Charlie's cherished buffalo calf

THE COMPANION PICTURE WAS LIKEWISE A DINNER
TABLE—BUT IT WAS SET IN A WELL-ORDERED COTTAGE,
AND AT IT CHARLIE AND I FACED EACH OTHER.

As I Was (1896), Charles M. Russell.
MONTANA HISTORICAL SOCIETY COLLECTION, HELENA, MONTANA (1986.06.04).

As I Am Now (1896), Charles M. Russell.
MONTANA HISTORICAL SOCIETY COLLECTION, HELENA, MONTANA (1986.06.05).

Two pictures, each worth a thousand words!

robe. Indian drawings were painted in soft colors on the skin side, depicting some incidents in Charlies' life. He had used this robe in his bed for years, so it was worn quite thin. But with an Indian blanket thrown on the floor against the back rest, it helped to make an interesting corner, as well as a comfortable seat.

A very shaky home-made easel and an ordinary kitchen chair completed the studio equipment.

———

Directly after we were married, Charlie made and sent to an old friend [Bill Rance, barkeep at the Silver Dollar Saloon in Great Falls] without comment twin drawings—both interiors. The first was a shack, grimy and cobweb-festooned. Skillets of bacon and potatoes were on the table where Charlie was eating. Boots, clothing, saddle and bridle, chips and all signs of a bachelor littered the floor.

The companion picture was likewise a dinner table—but it was set in a well-ordered cottage, and at it Charlie and I faced each other. [The silver service, a wedding gift from Bill Rance and the boys at the Silver Dollar, is prominently displayed.] The impression of comfort was unmistakable. It was

Russell Honeymoon Cabin. Photograph courtesy of Channing and Donna Hartelius.

In recent years, the Russells' Honeymoon Cottage was purchased and carefully cleaned and restored by a Cascade citizen, the late Gene Dwyer. It is now owned and being caringly preserved by Mr. and Mrs. Channing Hartelius.

Charlie's way of announcing to his friends that the old order of things had passed away, and the promise so made was daily redeemed in the improved character of his work. He lost none of his originality, none of his surpassing humor, but there was an element of earnestness in the mind of this child of the open West whose simple, honest nature could never be spoiled by conventionality. When a man like that had a hand that could spread his heart on a canvas, he was a genuine artist.

Christmas 1896

Things had gone very much awry with Charlie's work after we were married. He had no orders for pictures, and there was no chance in Cascade to meet buyers. But his credit was good, so we were eating regularly. Life was not too serious with us, as two saddle horses were kept picketed or in a pasture and did not need extra hay or grain.

The Missouri River gave us fish when we wanted to try for them, but Charlie didn't care much about fishing. He preferred to ride out to the buttes [especially Square Butte] or back into the hills where he could watch the changing shadows and colors on the rocks, the patterns of cloud upon the great valley below us. We watched ground squirrels and birds leading their busy lives. An ant hill kept us entertained for hours.

Thus Nature filled our days with joy, and civilization and those things which now seem most important never entered our minds to disturb us. Mother Nature was teaching her child true values, and he was a good student.

Charlie never lost the child-like spirit and love of the mysterious. He liked the Christmas festivities, when tissue paper was secretly rattled and the smell of oranges or the new paint of toys would give away their hiding-places.

Our first Christmas started with that spirit of mystery and secrecy, and we kept it throughout our lives. That first Christmas we had no money to spend and no place to spend it, if there had been any—just the little general mercantile store where one could buy overalls or bacon, but none of the fluffy Christmas things one sees nowadays.

We both needed many things. Among those we wanted most were warm slippers, for this shack-house of ours was not very warm except in summer. I bought for Charlie a pair of felt slippers and made a slipper bag out of black broadcloth. On one side of it I worked his initials with red silk, and mine on the other. I put the slippers in the case and hung it by his sock which he had put up for Santa Claus. My stocking was in another place to allow plenty of room for Santa to get around.

At four in the morning there was no more sleep for us. It was Christmas morning, our first Christmas, trotting in double harness!

I slipped out of bed, got my stocking and crawled back into bed. I found some nuts, an orange, and just the same kind of hard, little, bright-colored candies we had always had as children. And 'way down in the toe of the stocking I found a five dollar bill, while another package revealed to me a pair of felt slippers, the exact mates (only smaller) of those I have given my cowboy husband.

We were happy over that Christmas with nothing more than I've described, because the happiness came from within. Charlie was as pleased as if he had received a million-dollar gift. The simple things in life always did thrill him, and no one could live near him without taking on some of that child-like joy from little things.

Cascade

There were plenty of characters to study in Cascade, and very little escaped my cowboy husband.

One evening an old timer was celebrating. In doing so, he passed into oblivion. Several of his friends found him seated on an empty beer keg back of the saloon. Concerned lest he should move away or get lost, they nailed each side of his trousers to the keg. Now he was safe, they thought, and they went about their business.

In the afternoon, two kind-hearted gentlemen who were also a bit mellow thought they should take care of the poor old fellow. He should be taken home and put to bed. With each one taking him by an arm, they lifted him and guided his faltering steps homeward.

But he was heavy and unable to stand straight. He acted, indeed, like a man ready to make a big jump. One of the men thought he might be paralyzed and was all sympathy as they half-dragged the old timer down the street. He seemed to have hiccups in his knees, the helpers told each other; they must rub his legs.

It was then that they discovered the beer keg swinging on the seat of his trousers. It was a good thing his suspenders were stout!

WE RODE TO THE TOP OF [SQUARE] BUTTE
BACK OF CASCADE, WHERE WE COULD SEE
FOR MILES IN EVERY DIRECTION.

Charlie, Nancy and Monte in Cascade (1897), Cameron, William B. (photographer).
MONTANA HISTORICAL SOCIETY RESEARCH CENTER, HELENA, MONTANA, PHOTO ARCHIVES (944-681).

The Forepaugh & Sells Circus toured Montana only once, in early August 1896, before
Charlie and Nancy were married, and it did not play Great Falls; the Ringling Brothers
Circus toured Montana the next year and played Great Falls on June 4. Nancy misre-
membered the name of the circus, but not the excitement it caused. It was *"the first
big show the town has ever had,"* the Ringling Brothers tour book noted, *"and everyone within a radius of a hundred miles attended."* Charlie and Nancy could not afford
to go, but they saw the circus train pass through Cascade on its way to Great Falls, and
enjoyed a horseback ride instead. Such were the simple pleasures that Nancy recalled
so fondly in looking back on their first year of marriage.

The Circus
[June 1897]

THE FOURPAUGH THREE-RING CIRCUS was to be in Great Falls. All the posters had been out for weeks.

Charlie didn't talk much about it, for he knew the condition of our pocket book. But many of our friends around the little town of Cascade were very excited, and a number of them were going to see the circus.

Every little while someone would say, "Are you folks going?"

Charlie answered doubtfully, "I don't know . . . ."

When the day came, we learned from the railroad agent the exact hour the circus train was going through. Since we had not been able to raise any money, the best we could do was to get up at four o'clock in the morning and go out to the front of our little shack where we could watch the train pass. So, though we could not go to the circus in Great Falls, we had the thrill of seeing the circus train go through town.

After breakfast Charlie saddled the two horses, while I made a lunch which we tied onto the back of our saddles. We started out for the day. It was June. There had been much rain, and the river had outgrown her banks. We rode to the top of [Square] butte back of Cascade [shown on page 84], where we could see for miles in every direction.

In the Wake of the Buffalo Runners (1911), Charles M. Russell.
COURTESY OF A PRIVATE COLLECTION.

Nancy's statement that Charlie finished *all* paintings in his Great Falls studio may be close to accurate. However, there is no doubt that from 1907 onward he began many of his paintings at Bull Head Lodge on Lake McDonald, where the summer conditions inspired some of his finest oils. These could then be finished in the fall and winter in the Great Falls studio. In the first five summers spent at Bull Head Lodge, Charlie likely initiated many of the seventeen paintings of that period that Russell scholar Fred Renner deemed to be among his fifty greatest paintings. This prolific period culminated in the artist's 1911 masterpiece, *In the Wake of the Buffalo Runners*, shown above. (Nancy's rapturous description of the joys of life at Lake McDonald follows in a later chapter titled "Bull Head Lodge.")

Charles M. Russell, Fergus Mead, and Austin Russell
at Bull Head Lodge (1911), photographer unknown.
GILCREASE MUSEUM, TULSA, OKLAHOMA (TU2009.39.5748B-C).

Move to Great Falls
[September 1897]

T HERE WAS LITTLE CHANCE to get orders for pictures in such a small town [as Cascade,] so we moved to Great Falls where Charlie could meet a few travelers and get an occasional order.

Charles Schatzlein of Butte, Montana was a good friend. He had an art store and gave Charlie a good many orders, making it possible for us to pay our house rent and food, but Charlie said the grazing wasn't so good.

During one visit at our house, Mr. Schatzlein said, "Do you know, Russell, you don't ask enough for your pictures. That last bunch you sent me I sold one for enough to pay for six. I am paying you your price, but it's not enough. I think your wife should take hold of that end of the game and help you out."

From that time on, the prices of Charlie's work began to advance, until it was possible for us to live a little more comfortably.

In 1900 Charlie received a small legacy from his mother. This was the nest egg that started the home we lived in—and in which he died. After the cottage was completed and furnished [a little later], Charlie said, "I want a log studio some day, just a cabin like I used to live in."

That year, 1903, the studio was built on the lot adjoining the house. Charlie did not like the "mess" of building, so he took no more than a mild interest in the preparations. Then one day a neighbor asked, "What are you doing at your place, Russell, building a corral?"

That settled it with Charlie. He just thought the neighbors didn't want the cabin set down among civilized dwellings; he was convinced that they would get up a petition to prevent our building anything so unsightly as a log house in their midst. But deep in his heart he wanted that studio. It was the right kind of work shop for him.

He made no further comment, nor did he go near it until one evening Mr. Trigg, one of our dearest friends, came over and said, "Say, son, let's go see the new studio. That big stone fireplace looks good to me from the out-side. Show me what it's like from the inside."

Charlies looked at me to see if I had heard the request. The supper dishes must be washed; that was my job just then. So Charlie took Mr. Trigg out to his new studio that he himself had not yet entered. When they came back into the house, the dishes were all put away. Charlies was saying, "That's going to be a good shack for me. The bunch can come visit, talk and smoke while I paint."

From that day to the end of his life he loved that telephone-pole building more than any other place on earth, and after it was built, he never finished a painting anywhere else. [But after 1906 he often started many of his great works at Bull Head Lodge on Lake McDonald that he could then finish in Great Falls during the fall and winter periods.] The walls were hung with all kinds of things given him by Indian friends and his horse jewelry, as he called it, which had been accumulated on the range was as precious to him as a girl's jewel box to her.

One of Charlie's great joys was to give suppers that he himself cooked over the [studio's] fire[place] in a Dutch oven and frying pan. The invited guests were not to come near until the food was ready. There was usually bachelor bread, boiled beans, fried bacon—or if it was autumn, maybe some game and coffee—but the dessert must be dried apples.

A flour sack was tucked in Charlie's sash for an apron, and as he worked, great beads of perspiration would gather and roll down his face. When it was ready he would step to the door with a big smile and call out to us, "Come and get it!" There was a joyous light in his eyes when anyone asked for a second helping or praised the bread. When no more could be eaten, he would say, "Sure you got enough? Lots of grub here."

Then the coffee pot would be pushed aside, frying pan and Dutch oven pulled away from the fire. Charlie would get the "makins," Durham tobacco and white papers; then he sat on his heels among us as he rolled a cigarette with those long, slender fingers, lighted it, and in the smoke drifted back in his talk to times when there were very few, if any, white women in Montana. It was Nature's country.

[Nancy concludes] If that cabin could only tell what [stories] those log walls have heard!

Charles Russell's Studio.
PHOTO COURTESY OF THE C.M. RUSSELL MUSEUM.

Great Falls—Our First Real Money—Second Christmas
1897 and 1898

THE SECOND CHRISTMAS after we were married, Charlie had quite a lot of work to do. He painted a 6' x 4' canvas called "The Last Stand," for which he received one hundred five dollars. The man who bought it later raffled it off for a dollar a chance, but I do not know how many chances were sold. [In the Appendix on page 189, Nancy notes that a banker's one-dollar raffle ticket won the painting, which was sold three years later to another banker for five thousand dollars. She was ever alert to art pricing data.]

The Park Hotel had a special Christmas dinner, and Charlie made an original water color on one hundred twenty-five menu cards. For this he received twenty dollars [only 16¢ for each image]. Right there we had a real fuss. He had worked days on them, and I thought he should have a least as much as the cook and waiters would get per day. He thought so, too, but did not have the courage to ask for enough for us to live on and save a cent.

But in spite of this, we were fairly prosperous. Out of the Christmas orders we had managed to save seventy-five dollars. I hid the money in an Indian leggin which decorated one of our living-room walls.

We had a four-room house whose cellar was always full of water. Charlie said it would make a good place to put up ice in winter and raise ducks in summer.

It was here that we lived when Father Russell first visited us. He came to see who Charlie had married. There was a question in the minds of the family, and seeing the girl was the only way to settle it. I must have passed inspection, for Father always made me feel that I was truly his daughter.

We were happy in those four rooms. Charlie painted in what we called our dining-room. It was a hard place for him to work, as it had a west window, but fortunately he worked very early in the morning and played afternoons, making it possible for him to do as well as he did.

One day we met a woman who wanted a water color of a steamboat

THE PARK HOTEL HAD A SPECIAL CHRISTMAS DINNER,
AND CHARLIE MADE AN ORIGINAL WATER COLOR
ON ONE HUNDRED TWENTY-FIVE MENU CARDS.

Park Hotel 1897 Christmas dinner menu:
Cowboy and Indian Handshake, Charles M. Russell.
PETRIE COLLECTION.

Park Hotel 1897 Christmas dinner menu:
Buffalo at Riverside, Charles M. Russell.
BIG SKY COLLECTION: LARRY AND LEANNE PETERSON.

These individually illustrated menu cards are among the less than a dozen believed to have survived from the Park Hotel 1897 Christmas dinner. Nancy's point to Charlie was that it was crazy to produce them for only 16¢ each. Interestingly, in recent auction markets their rarity has been confirmed by individual purchases ranging from $15,000 to $25,000. As Austin Russell observed about his favorite uncle, *"If left to himself, Charlie was not very practical; he would devote just as much care to things not meant to sell."*

stopped by buffalo crossing the Missouri River. The finished piece of work was a beauty, and we thought it should bring a good price. Charlie hoped the buyer would pay twenty-five dollars. We needed hay for the horses, and I wanted a new cook stove. So I asked if I couldn't deliver the picture.

"Now, Mame, if you ask more than twenty-five dollars for that picture, she won't take it, and we need the money."

But our lady saw the beauty of the picture and was much pleased. She asked, "How much does Mr. Russell want for it?"

With a choking sensation, I said, "Thirty-five dollars."

"Just wait; I will give you a check."

Glory be! I had ten dollars toward the new cook stove. Charlie got as great a thrill out of that piece of paper as he did when I handed him a check for thirty thousand dollars in 1926, when he quietly said, "I can't read so many figures. What do they say?"

ONE DAY WE MET A WOMAN WHO WANTED
A WATER COLOR OF A STEAMBOAT STOPPED BY
BUFFALO CROSSING THE MISSOURI RIVER.

Steam Boat Days (1886), Charles M. Russell.
PETRIE COLLECTION.

Steam Boat Days is a sketch done by Charlie back in about 1886 depicting just such an occasion as Nancy indicates was commissioned in 1897 by the lady purchaser of Russell's watercolor version of the event. That person may have been the wife of Great Falls' first mayor and founder of the city, Paris Gibson. During the early summer, run-off of melting snow from higher elevations limited the ability of steamboats loaded with supplies from St. Louis to navigate all the way upriver to Fort Benton. This was especially the case as the season wore on. This also enabled large buffalo herds to more easily ford the Missouri River at a growing number of points. Thus, incidents as depicted in *Steam Boat Days* became more commonplace as spring turned to summer.

Waiting for the Herd to Cross is the finished piece delivered and "priced on a unilaterally revised basis" by Nancy. This composition can be viewed as the genesis of the idea for what many consider Russell's greatest masterpiece executed sixteen years later. If one removes the paddle wheeler and advances the bison herd up onto the Missouri River's west bank, the scene foreshadows *When the Land Belonged to God* (see page 45).

Waiting for the Herd to Cross (1898), Charles M. Russell.
PETRIE COLLECTION.

Bronze bust of Charlie Russell
from John Marchand's plaster model (n.d.).
PETRIE COLLECTION.

Smoking Up (modeled 1903; cast 1904),
Charles M. Russell.
PETRIE COLLECTION.

Here Nancy confirms the valuable contributions by John Marchand, Will Crawford, and Bill Hart in helping her convince Charlie to pursue opportunities in New York. While John Marchand never achieved the art market appreciation or financial success of Russell, he was an accomplished illustrator in his own right. Additionally, he played an important role in Charlie's artistic development by exposing him to his own illustration techniques as well as those of a dozen or more New York–based artists, including Ed Borein, Maynard Dixon, Charles Schreyvogel, and others that Nancy identifies later. When Marchand died, Charlie called attention to the news in a letter to Borein on May 1, 1921. Earlier (1905) Russell and Marchand had created and exchanged busts of one another. The bronze shown above was cast from John Marchand's plaster model of Charlie.

In fact, Charlie Russell did execute in New York his first sculpture to be cast in bronze, *Smoking Up*, showcasing his appreciation for the skills he developed during his 1904 visit. As noted by Fred Renner, this sculpture became his most popular posthumously reproduced bronze composition.

Charlie's Trail Leads Him
Into a Lighter Mood

IT TOOK [MORE THAN] A LITTLE PERSUASION to convince Charlie that we should go to see his friends in New York. Every letter from them had been urging him to come east. "There is work waiting for you here. With the help of Bill Hart and (John) Marchand and Will Crawford to introduce you to people who want illustrations or covers for magazine, you can also model something to be cast in plaster and later in bronze."

Charlie would never have gone east without the friendship of these fellows he had met in the West. He liked them; he felt that they liked him, so it was a joy to visit them in the country where they lived.

Many of the trails leading to Charlie's successes were blazed by those boys. Bill Hart, for instance, knew a man desirous of owning a Charlie Russell painting. The meeting was arranged and the picture was ordered.

Upon its completion, Charlie and I discussed the price he should ask for it. Charlie, as usual, was fearful of asking too much. His argument was that we were a long way from home and needed whatever amount we could get. He thought [about] one hundred fifty dollars should be the upper limit.

The buyer was much interested in the finished piece of work. "What is your price?" he asked.

Charlie opened his mouth and looked at me. This was no time to hesitate, so I spoke up at once. "Four hundred dollars!"

There was complete silence for a few seconds, then the gentleman said, "I'll take it."

Charlie nearly strangled, coughed, rolled and lit a cigarette.

When we were alone, he asked, "How could you do it?" and after a pause, "Well, after this, I'll do the work and you'll do the selling."

Our buyer was very pleased with his purchase, and he made it the first step toward a successful trip East for us [as will become clear later].

[Thus] our visit in New York became [almost] a yearly event for us.

Mr. Crawford [and Marchand's] studio there was Charlie's to work in.

His Heart Sleeps (1911), Charles M. Russell.
BUFFALO BILL CENTER OF THE WEST, CODY, WYOMING: WHITNEY WESTERN ART MUSEUM (89.60.1).

This poignant oil painting, a treasured gift to Nancy, was accompanied by a short
poem Charlie wrote about an Indian burial scaffold "at river's brink." Nancy intended
to include it and eight other poems by Charlie in her book.

His Heart Sleeps

No flowers deck his resting place,
No marble marks the spot.
But nature loves her children—
Her child is not forgot.

Oft-times she rocks his cradle
Which hangs at river's brink.
Her waters hum his lullaby,
Where great herds come to drink.

His God, the sun, rides guard for him
And throws his golden light,
The moon with all her children
Watches o'er him through the night.
—Charles M. Russell

This was fine, because Charlie had no chance to get homesick. The boys who came to the studio thought a good deal as Charlie did.

Charlie loved to get a crowd of artists together and have them all talk about their own work. He invited them to visit him in Montana, where he said he could show them the country. Even if the life had changed, he could tell them about it. He tried to keep the old order of things alive, in spite of the changing [nature] of the frontier life. He consistently urged the artists to do their best to preserve the characters in history. He felt that there was much more to be done than there were men with the desire to do it. He kept no secrets from his fellow artists but took joy in telling them how he worked, how he never overlooked an opportunity to study animals and people from life.

The following is an example of what Charlie meant:

His drawings of the Indian pony and the small cow horse of the prairie were perfection. Their slim legs, deep chests and short backs were like the build of their ancestors which the Spanish brought into Old Mexico many years ago.

The buffalo or bison drawn by Charlie were not all one age and size like those seen at the zoo. Unlike Charlie, many painters had never had the opportunity of seeing them in their wild state. In the Louvre [in Paris] we saw a buffalo hunt. The Indian hunters were wearing huge eagle feather war bonnets. Their horses were the Norman type. The buffalo herd were all bulls, very fat, with long tails flagged. The chase was through a country dotted with the slender poplar trees of France. The painting may have been perfect in technique, but there was not one authentic detail. Perhaps that fact did not matter to the average person, but it was very important to Charlie.

Few artists have had his opportunity to get [so] near to nature as God created it. On one occasion [probably in 1919], when he had finished about half of his work on a buffalo hunt, he said to me, "Let's go over to the [Flathead] Reservation and see those hump-back cows."

Charlie [in May 1909] had helped corral the buffalo when the Canadian government bought the Allard herd and moved it to Wainwright, Canada. After the greater part of the animals had been moved, the United States government set aside a range for those that were left. They had to be under fence, as their grazing country was thrown open to settlers.

Pablo Buffalo Hunt (1909), Charles M. Russell.
BIG SKY COLLECTION: LARRY AND LEANNE PETERSON.

Here Nancy is referencing the so-called Pablo buffalo roundups of 1908 and 1909 where about seventy-five riders moved several hundred bison over a long distance to a rail-head for shipment to Canada. The latter was the only party willing to take the last of them. This experience involved moving at considerable personal risk in and among the buffalo herd, as shown here in Charlie's watercolor. Though he witnessed the roundup in the fall of 1908, he actually rode with the drivers the following spring. His personal involvement speaks to why major oils such as *Wounded* (1909), *The Surround* (1911), *Fighting Meat* (1918), *The Buffalo Hunt* (No. 39), and *The Buffalo Hunt* (No. 40)—both painted in 1919—are among the artist's most breathtaking works on this subject. The first owner of the *Pablo Buffalo Hunt* was Howard Douglas, who Nancy also cites as favorably assessing Charlie's herding skills. He was the superintendent of the Banff Park and a good friend of Russell's. The painting above depicts Russell witnessing another cowboy's up-close encounter with a recalcitrant buffalo bull.

The Buffalo Hunt (No. 39) (1919), Charles M. Russell. Oil on canvas;
Amon Carter Museum of American Art, Fort Worth, Texas,
AMON G. CARTER COLLECTION (1961.146).

THE PAINTING FINISHED AFTER THAT VISIT NOW BELONGS TO MR. WILL ROGERS.

One can easily imagine why Russell wanted a personal reminder of what "running buffalo" was all about. His last two paintings produced in 1919 are widely considered to be among his finest such works.

What a happy time Charlie had on that trip! He handled wild buffalo just as he had handled wild cattle in his cow puncher days. Mr. [Howard] Douglas, a Canadian official [commissioner of Dominion Parks at Banff, Alberta], said that Charlie corralled more buffalo single-handed than anyone there [but not without risk, as the adjacent lower image that includes a self-portrait of Russell suggests]. He was in his glory. The Pon de Rell [Pend d'Oreille] country was not over-fenced. Many wild horses roamed the hills, and on the open range Indians, riding their best horses, helped gather the buffalo.

This was like a post-graduate course on moving Buffalo for Charlie, since he had been so surely a part of this kind of [cowboy] life in the eighties. The six weeks' work, day and night, brought him untold joy; every action was stamped in his memory for the balance of his life [especially the close calls with bison adventures]. Yet he wanted to see the herd again while he was painting the hunt [which proved to be one of his last and greatest].

And Mother Nature was kind to him on that trip! When he arrived at the range, about two hundred head were down near the fence—cows, calves, young bulls and the big old fellows with long chaps and whiskers, grazing or just walking about.

Charlie went up the fence to talk to them. After he had had a good look at [them in a] quiet [state], he said, "I want to see you fellows run."

He waved his hat and hollered as he would at wild cattle. Away they went, up and over the grassy slope and out of sight.

The painting [*The Buffalo Hunt* (No. 39)] finished after that visit now belongs to Mr. Will Rogers. [Subsequently, it along with *The Buffalo Hunt* (No. 40) was purchased by Amon Carter, and No. 39 is still in the Amon Carter Museum Collection.]

But that was the sort of lesson-from-life he wanted to convey to those artists close to him in New York . . . .

One day when Charlie and Bill Hart were out together they were somewhere given a Canadian quarter. They went in to the bar of the Waldorf-Astoria for a drink. This quarter they have as part payment to the bar tender, who refused to take it. Thereupon the boys decided he would take it, so they kept on drinking.

On his return to the Studio, Charlie was asked why he had been gone so long and why he looked so queer [i.e., odd].

The Last Laugh (1916), Charles M. Russell.
PETRIE COLLECTION.

As Nancy's comments indicate, Charlie's appendectomy experience was not pleasant. In a 1908 illustrated letter to his friend Bob Benn in Kalispell he admits, *"since the Doctor trimmed me"* am *"still sum sore."*

This edition of *The Last Laugh*, a *memento mori* in bronze, was given to Charlie's doctor who, Nancy tells us, advised Charlie after his appendectomy to cut back on drinking and smoking if he did not want to die prematurely. Ironically, it was that same doctor who ultimately died from lung cancer, and the discoloration of the patina on this small bronze indicates that, as intended, it was heavily used as an ashtray.

Charlie's painful recovery from his 1907 operation seems to have given him a phobia about surgery. Almost twenty years later, he persistently procrastinated in seeking an operation to remove his oversize goiter. Most unfortunately, it was this surgery at the Mayo Clinic in the summer of 1926 that, while successful in itself, revealed a much advanced deterioration of Charlie's cardiovascular system.

"We got drunk," said he, "trying to pass a Canadian quarter, and I still have it, so I did not do as I intended."

Next year (1907) Charlie had his appendix removed.

After the anesthetic the doctor had to administer a heart stimulant.

"If you had had a few more drinks and cigarettes," the doctor [Albert Forrest Longeway] later said to him, "you wouldn't have lived through this."

After that there was no more hard liquor for Charlie, and not so many smokes. But he didn't think that everyone had to quit just because he had.

Sometimes he said, "I'm water-logged with Lythia water," for it was that which he substituted for hard liquor when he was with his drinking friends. It takes a powerful will to stop drinking. Charlie had that will, yet retained all his drinking friends, too.

Charlie and Bill Hart had many happy hours together, and I was usually lucky enough to go with them. When we first saw the ocean, Charlie dug for clams which were later carried back to the city in Bill's handkerchief.

[On April 20,] 1907 Charlie wrote this letter to our neighbor, Mr. Trigg:

"Friend Trigg:

I received your letter and was plenty glad to here [hear] from you.

New York is as noisy as ever an, baring [the] Bronks [sic zoo] and Central Park, I don't find much to amuse me. Last Sunday, we went to the beach an took a look at the Atlantic. This little strip of water aint changed much. I guess she's roling about the same as she did when old Hudson an his Dutch crew sighted shore but I don't think old Henery would know the place if he'd see her now. The camp's bilt up considerbul since he was here an ther's more saviges. I was out at Bronks [Bronx Zoo] a fiew days ago an stayed all day. They have quite a fiew new animals since I was [last] here. This is one of them. Ain't he sweet? If it's right that man came from monkey, I savy where Baldy the bar-keep got his complection. Of corse, this is with all do respect to the monk.

Well, Trigg, as talking is easeyer for me than writen an I expect to see you pretty soon, I'll close with best wishes to all."

One evening Bill Hart, Will Rogers, Charlie Russell and I [Nancy] went to dinner at a little restaurant. After we were seated we heard someone say,

DO YOU REALIZE WHAT AN INFLUENCE CHARLIE HAD ON MY PICTURE WORK?

Bill Hart's assertion to Nancy about Charlie's influence on him as an actor is revealing of this theatrical performer and silent film actor's high respect. The friendship between Charlie Russell and William S. Hart was deep and enduring. When Hart published his autobiography in 1929, it contained Charlie's portrait of him painted in 1908. That image underscores Nancy's comments about Charlie's talented ability to thoroughly capture intricate cowboy equipment details.

Portrait of William S. Hart on Horseback (n.d.),
CHARLES M. RUSSELL. WILLIAM S. HART MUSEUM,
NATURAL HISTORY MUSEUM OF LOS ANGELES COUNTY (A.7211.58-1717).

DO YOU REMEMBER HOW MUCH YOU PAID FOR THE PAINTING, 'WHERE THE NOSE OF A HORSE BEATS THE EYES [SIC] OF MAN?'

When the Nose of a Horse Beats the Eyes of a Man (1916), Charles M. Russell.
WILLIAM S. HART MUSEUM, NATURAL HISTORY MUSEUM OF LOS ANGELES COUNTY (A.7211.58-1718).

Bill Hart was a very special friend of the Russells, but due to economic realities Nancy did not offer a *"friends and family discount price"* for big paintings by Charlie. This 30x48-inch masterpiece painting is a prize holding in the William S. Hart Collection of the Natural History Museum of Los Angeles.

As Charlie Russell knew well: *"The horse, like most animals, uses his nose before his eyes and is often frightened before he has seen what has scared him. The smell of a bear will stampede most horses."*

"I know that's Will Rogers and Bill Hart, but who in Hell is the other old guy with them?"

They were like boys together. On our visit to a five-masted schooner which was setting sail for Australia, they cast off when the ship started on her long journey.

Bill Hart gave us dozens of theater tickets. They were a great treat to his western friends who knew so little about a big city and [had] so few funds to spend.

When we left for home, the trunk had to be transferred from the hotel to the depot. When I went to check it, I found that there was a dollar charge. Since I couldn't get at my money easily, I asked Charlie, who as usual had only twenty-five cents—his limit!

Bill—good scout that he was—came to the rescue. Many years later I learned that that dollar had been all he had with him, and he had walked miles back to his apartment. I'll wager that he was glad his sagebrush friends had departed for the country where they were better known!

Bill asked me the other day, "Do you realize what an influence Charlie had on my picture work? When I'd start a picture, I could just look out in front and see what Charlie would want to do with a picture like that, and I would try to follow that."

Charlie drew in detail the equipment the cowboy in the eighties would have worn in the West. In that way Bill Hart got perfect detail in his costuming.

It was my turn to ask him, "Do you remember how much you paid for the painting, 'Where the nose of a horse beats the eyes [sic] of man?' "

Bill said, "Sure, I remember. Charlie was so mad! He didn't think I should pay so much for it. But I got a grand picture, and I think it was worth the money I paid."

"We were mighty broke at that time," I told Bill, "and the sale of that picture gave us money to get home and straighten out some of our expenses . . . ."

The Lazy KY Ranch house, 1910. Left to right: Con and Claudia Price, Henry "Pike" Webster
(the son of an old Great Falls friend of the Russells who owned a ranch in Canada 12 miles to the north),
Charlie Russell, Philip Goodwin, and Leslie Price. It is likely Nancy Russell took the picture.
C.M. RUSSELL MUSEUM, GREAT FALLS, MONTANA, GIFT OF RICHARD FLOOD II (975-12-0149.17).

In 1904, Cornelius E. (Con) Price, an old cowboy friend of Charlie's, filed on a squatter's claim on Kicking Horse Creek five miles below the Canadian border, where he started the Lazy KY Ranch. Charlie, having filed a claim of his own on an adjacent property, on January 1, 1906, became co-owner of the Lazy KY. Con ran the day-to-day operations until drought forced them to dissolve the partnership in 1910—but not before Charlie, Nancy, and their summer guest, wildlife artist Philip R. Goodwin, made a farewell visit to the ranch in September.

The following passage, attributed to Russell's cowboy friend Belknap (Ballie) Buck, the son of a Gros Ventre and Assiniboine mother and a white father, provides an interesting perspective: *"I made one more trip into the Falls [Great Falls] around Christmas. . . . We went to [Albert J.] Trigg's saloon [The Brunswick] and shot the bull. [Present were Charlie Russell, Teddy Blue Abbott, Johnny Lea, Johnny Brinkman, and Con Price. Buck had just been promoted to running a cattle outfit in Canada.] They were pleased that the Circle [Circle C outfit] was sending me north, but we all knew that [in] times like these [we] would be further apart. Charlie was married by then so he headed home sort of early. He tried to keep Nancy happy."*

Kickin' Hoss Ranch
(West Butte, Montana)
1904

CHARLIE WENT UP TO SEE how things were going and found [another special friend from his cowboy days and ranch co-owner] Con Price, making an irrigation ditch. Con, no better a farmer than Charlie, found this as great a difficulty as an engineer might find a far more vast project than one small ditch running along a steep bank.

Con had made what they called a "go-devil" (a triangular shaped device) that required a human ballast to scrape the dirt. This ditch amounted to little more than turning over the sod. Con asked Charlie to help him; his contribution was to ride the "go-devil" to help weigh it down. The team consisted of two saddle horses: one an outlaw, given to Con as a gift.

[Using his common sense] Charlie was in doubt about riding it, for when he saw how it acted, he thought it wouldn't be very safe to ride behind the horses, [given] that the go-devil would [probably] tip over.

But Con convinced him that it was perfectly safe, so he got on the "go-devil" with Con. They had negotiated about fifty feet of this ditch when the one horse jumped and kicked over the traces, turning the "go-devil" over.

Charlie and Con both fell off and rolled down into the creek.

Charlie Filing a Claim
to the Land at Gold Butte –
1905

WHEN CON PRICE TOOK CHARLIE to Gold Butte, they went to file a desert[ed] claim [on a parcel that became Charlie's contribution to ownership of the Lazy KY Ranch].

Con and Charlie had to go fourteen miles on horseback. Con got what he thought was a gentle horse for Charlie, gave Charlie the bridle [and] reins and turned his back. At the sound of a strange noise, he looked about to see Charlie flat on his back with his left foot fast to the stirrup and the horse dragging him, while striking at him with his front foot. Just as Con ran to catch the horse, Charlie's foot had worked loose from the stirrups.

Con later related this story:

"Charlie asked me if this was one of my pets that I had given him to ride!

"I told him that the horse hadn't bucked for four or five years, and I thought that he had got over it.

"He said that that would make him feel good, [actually now] knowing that the horse had been a bad bucker.

"He didn't want to ride out of trot all day, no matter how much I tried to urge him to speed up, because he knew that horse was just waiting for him to go into a lope and then would start bucking."

Charlie told [me] later that Con had [guaranteed] the horse to be gentle, insisting that he didn't buck. This [assurance] reminded Charlie of a horse once sold in Great Falls, guaranteed to be a lady's horse—but he [then actually] killed two men in Butte afterward!

The Horse Trade at the Price-Russell Ranch
[The Lazy KY] 1909

Con [Price] had met [Jake] DeHart at Choteau and told him that he was looking for a horse that would make a rope horse; he would give him a good trade for a horse of that description. DeHart had a horse that Russ had said you couldn't tell whether it was a "mountain or a hoss."

Con traded DeHart twelve head of horses for this one.

Charlie found no one at the ranch when he [next] came there. Con was away riding. The big horse was standing in the corral, and when Con came home, Charlie asked him where he had got that "mountain of beauty."

Con told him about the trade.

"Well, he's a good sleeper," commented Charlie. "I looked at him for an hour in the corral, and he never moved an ear!"

Charlie looked at Con in a puzzled way; he couldn't figure him out, until Con spoke up unconcernedly:

"I traded him twelve head of locoed hosses for this one."

[A locoed horse is one that has been brain drugged by eating locoweed. It remains a serious problem for ranchers in the West even today. Since full recovery from eating this plant is unlikely, Con's trade was an effective way to shed twelve potentially unsolvable problems!]

April 24, 1930

Mr. Philip R. Goodwin
Lewis and Grove Streets
Mamaroneck, New York

Dear Philip:

I am sending by express a copy of Charlie's book "Good Medicine", together with his illustrated letters loaned me by you.

This book is a gift from me in appreciation for your goodness in letting me use your treasures to help make the book what it is.

I know there are many things in that book that will make you back-track to Montana and your visit with Charlie.

I hope it will give you joy.

Sincerely,

Nancy C. Russell

P. S. When you notify me of the receipt of the book at the same time will you please acknowledge it to Mr. H. E. Maule, Doubleday Doran Company, Garden City, N.Y.

Note: Four illustrated letters returned.

R/W

Letter to Philip R. Goodwin, April 24, 1930, Nancy C. Russell.
PETRIE COLLECTION.

As the letter above suggests, Nancy maintained a good friendship with Phil Goodwin even after Charlie died. Both Goodwin and another of Charlie's artist friends, Ed Borein, were especially helpful as Nancy worked to assemble the illustrated letters for the publication of *Good Medicine*.

Philip Goodwin and the
Run-away Horse
[1910]

PHILIP [R. GOODWIN, A VISITING ARTIST,] and Charlie went to the Kickin' Hoss Ranch; they had also been over to the [Frank] Webster ranch in Canada. Goodwin wanted to see some western life, that he might revive in his memory what he already knew. There was no better place than that of Con Price, so that is where they landed.

Goodwin wanted to ride a good horse, and Con was famous for his good horses. When Con asked Charlie if Goodwin could ride such a horse, Charlie replied that he thought he could ride [about] "average." They gave Goodwin a good, high-lifed [i.e., spirited] horse.

Goodwin mounted the horse, leaned forward and pressed his knees against the horse, which was the signal for him to go. They were beside a line about forty feet wide, with a wire fence on either side. The horse started on a dead run right along the wire fence and ran about a quarter of a mile. With every jump he looked as though his leg were going to hit the wire.

We were all powerless to do anything, and we didn't know what to do. I hollered, "Do something! Catch that horse!"

Mr. Price took after Goodwin on another horse, but Goodwin had turned. His horse was coming back at the same fierce speed, the man's legs flapped so that he kicked the horse at every jump.

Price managed to catch the horse and lead him back.

Price later described the confusion:

"After the excitement was over, Mrs. Russell almost collapsed, and we gave up the ride that we all were going to take. She went in the house and lay down. Charlie and I walked around and tried to think of some way to ease the excitement. Finally he went into the room where Mrs. Russell was and tried to explain that it was a mistake on his part and mine; that we didn't know the horse would run away with Goodwin and didn't know Goodwin wasn't familiar with that kind of horse. She told Charlie that we were both

Philip R. Goodwin and Charles Marion Russell Riding,
from illustrated letter, CMR to Philip Goodwin, November 1910.
STARK MUSEUM OF ART, ORANGE, TEXAS (31.11.5)

Charles Marion Russell and Philip R. Goodwin Visiting on their Horseback Ride,
from illustrated letter, CMR to Philip Goodwin, November 1910.
STARK MUSEUM OF ART, ORANGE, TEXAS (31.11.4)

These two watercolor sketches depict Charlie's ride with Phil Goodwin from the Lazy KY Ranch to Great Falls. They accompanied a letter Charlie wrote to Goodwin in late November 1910, which is also in the Stark Museum of Art collection.

crazy. And she wouldn't talk to him about it. Charlie came outside and said that he guessed [Nancy believed that] we'd played Hell [on Goodwin]! He said Nancy had asked him, "What could I tell that boy's mother if anything should happen to him?"

Charlie and Mr. Price thought they should somehow square themselves with Philip Goodwin. So they gave to him a gun which was prized as a relic and in which he was very interested.

Charlie said that Goodwin held it in a scabbard on his shoulder all the hundred thirty-five miles to Great Falls. He got there with it all right, but one shoulder was a good deal lower than the other when they arrived at the end of their journey.

[Nancy's description of Con's shrewdness in the previously described 12-for-1 horse trade perhaps puts her suspicions about his periodic wiliness into a different light, and justifies her skepticism about Con and Charlie's professed innocence in choosing a "less than gentle" horse for Phil Goodwin. That said, in his book *Trails I Rode*, written after both Goodwin and Nancy were dead, Con still insisted that the incident was not intentionally orchestrated. But he also admitted, "While Charlie and I were around the rest of the bunch we had to look very solemn and sorry, but when we got alone we would have a big laugh." After all, Goodwin was unharmed and old cowboys always enjoyed initiating a tenderfoot.]

Note to Mr. and Mrs. Calvert on birch bark (detail) (1906), Charles M. Russell.
PETRIE COLLECTION.

This 1906 greeting card on birch bark sent to George Calvert and family, close Great Falls friends who became regular guests at Bull Head Lodge, shows Charlie and Nancy rowing to their new cabin on Lake McDonald. They are towing a second boat loaded with supplies. That first year it was called Kootenai Lodge, but as Brian Dippie surmises, Nancy quickly realized the branding value of renaming it Bull Head Lodge to further underscore Charlie's trademarked signature with a buffalo skull for his paintings. (See page 129.) The name change also eliminated any possible confusion with another Kootenai lodge owned by a Russell friend at nearby Swan Lake outside the park.

Philip R. Goodwin, Untitled (Charles Russell's cabin at Lake McDonald, Montana), about 1907. Denver Art Museum: William Sr. and Dorothy Harmsen Collection, 2009.321.
PHOTOGRAPHY COURTESY OF DENVER ART MUSEUM.

This sketch of Nancy proudly viewing Bull Head Lodge (subsequently enveloped by Glacier National Park) was drawn by Phil Goodwin on his first visit there in 1907 (he returned in 1910). Nancy's fond memories of Charlie's and her time together are evident as her writing aims to wax poetical. The year 1907 was when Charlie and Goodwin incised a series of images on the face of the cabin's fireplace. This drawing was not used in that effort but was one of about a dozen studies done by Goodwin likely in preparation for that project. These drawings are now part of the Harmsen Collection at the Denver Art Museum.

Bull Head Lodge
[subsequently enveloped by Glacier National Park]

[CHARLIE] HAD A STUDIO [next to the cabin] in the mountains and, as I remember, these are some of the things he saw and loved:

But you will have to leave the heat, noise and turmoil of civilization behind you, let yourself in fancy feel the soft breast of Mother earth under you as you follow the trails that lead into the shade of trees God has planted and nourished as no man could.

Your feet seem to cling to the ground, which is covered with cedar and pine needles. There is no familiar sound. The hush is like that of a great cathedral just before the organ tells you the choir is coming. The soul of you seems to listen as the voices of nature approach, first softly, lest they frighten you away. The talk of tumbling water hidden by ferns starts the song; the clear, sweet notes of birds join with the chatter of a saucy, bright-eyed squirrel questioning the human intruder.

You may find a spot where the sun peeps through. There, with shiny silver thread, Mrs. Spider is weaving a web. It glitters like strings of minute jewels as the soft breeze swings the branches that hold it.

In the decayed wood and leaf mold a cluster of ghost flowers (Indian Pipe), nestles pearly-white against the earth. And without a knowing why, your eyes follow a deer trail to that spot just beyond a clump of ferns in a sunny glade where a doe pauses with her two spotted babies, their great soft eyes questioning your friendship. If you do not move, they will quietly disappear into the shadowy woods.

A porcupine may bar your way for a few seconds as he crosses the path. Fearless he is, because he knows that all things respect the weapons that rattle as he moves along, bear-like. Take a large handkerchief, flip it across his back, and he still gives you some souvenir quills for an ornament on your hat.

Now your eyes and ears are awake. Your nose tells you balsam is near. As the trail curves downward into more open places between the trees, a fragrance, defying description, comes to you. The earth is covered with a running vine and, like a veil covering the green trailers, is a lavender-pink

CLOUDS THROW THEIR PROTECTING FOLDS
AROUND THESE PEAKS. . . . THE SUN WILL THEN
GATHER THEM TO ITSELF, MAKING LIVING COLOR
TO BE REFLECTED BY MOUNTAINS AND LAKE

Fallen Tree at Lake McDonald (1917), Charles M. Russell.
PETRIE COLLECTION.

Ginger Renner told a group of C.M. Russell Museum board members visiting Bull
Head Lodge in 2008 an interesting background story about this C.M. Russell painting
of a fallen tree. Fred Renner had acquired it, and before they were married Ginger
had owned a companion piece of the same subject by Maynard Dixon. The two works
dated to when both artists were painting "plein air" together in 1917 down at the
water's edge on Lake McDonald below Bull Head Lodge. This may have been one
of those occasions when Charlie was confronting the difficulty of painting "shining
water."

mist of tiny, bell-shaped flowers giving you their perfume. Your feet will not carry you past until the fragrance of these twin flowers has filled your lungs and heart with its sweetness, unforgettably [noted] . . . .

Slowly you move on to that stronger light just below where the mountain maple has grown thick and the wild hollyhock waves. You see a lacy mountain spray and bear grass which has sent forth its stately white plume to fascinate you. There is the trickle of a cool spring pushing its way through moss and ferns under great logs fallen long years ago; nature has covered them with a mantle of green, like a miniature forest.

Follow on to the sunlight you have seen reflected by the waters of Lake McDonald. Wooded mountains shelter it, pushing their rocky crests high above timberline, nourishing bright glaciers that gleam in the blue waters of the lake. Clouds throw their protecting folds around these peaks to give you time to think, and when you can once more endure [to] stand their beauty, they drift away. The sun will then gather them to itself, making living color to be reflected by mountains and lake—a tremulous pink and rose-lavendar and cobalt blue, against an apple-green horizon . . . .

Twin birches reach out to the lake. On one of them a buffalo skull is fastened. A log, drifted in with the high water, has lodged among the willow and maple brushes near the birches. Here you can rest in the shade and see clearly in all directions.

On the sloping mountain-side you can see, snuggled down among the trees, a brown log cabin with a shake roof. It cannot be seen from the surface of the lake, because the scars men would make on the timber during its building have been covered by stain the color of pine needles on the earth. There is not a jarring note about the cabin.

Charlie did not want to cut the big trees growing near the cabin site so [we] built the steps to the porch between the three that grew in a group at the front. The floor and landing were made of logs hewed with an ax to make rough boards which were cut enough to keep the trees from touching the floor, making a very artistic entrance to the cabin that is stained to match the forest [as can be seen in Goodwin's depiction of Nancy viewing the cabin, bottom page 124]. A hand-made easel with its canvas reflects nature's color. Near it, in the corner, a camp stool leans against the porch rail for the painter [to use].

If you were close enough, you could see over the doorway a kind of hood,

I CAN'T PAINT THE LAKE. I'VE TRIED TO, BUT IT'S TOO MUCH FOR ME.

Bull Head Lodge privacy screen featuring decoration by Kathryn Leighton (1925).
C.M. RUSSELL MUSEUM, GREAT FALLS, MONTANA, GIFT OF LARRY AND LEANNE PETERSON (996.27.6).

Lake McDonald Looking North (ca 1925-27), Kathryn Leighton.
PETRIE COLLECTION.

Given Charlie's reservations about painting "shining water," it is striking to see the artist Kathryn Leighton's willingness to take on this challenge from the shore of Bull Head Lodge. While Charlie probably never saw her completed painting, he did see her study done on the Bull Head Lodge privacy screen when she stayed with the Russells in 1925. That was also the year that Charlie introduced her to officials at the Great Northern Railway. The following year she became employed by that enterprise to create paintings designed to draw tourists to Glacier National Park. Leighton's painting is a cherished gift to the Petrie Collection by the late Steve Rose, founder of the Charlie Russell Riders.

like the roof, to protect a buffalo skull which is the emblem of the camp. In signing a piece of work, Charlie always drew a buffalo skull with his name. [Ever the marketer, Nancy states,] That is why we called the camp "Bull Head Lodge," for a stranger would know by this emblem that Charlie was the owner.

Charlie Russell, artist and lover of nature, sat on a log near me. He looked at the mountains and shining water of the lake and said, "I can't paint the lake. I've tried to, but it's too much for me. There are some things Ma Nature won't let man copy, and this is one of them. I've read where some men say they can improve on nature. I don't think [of it] that way. If it could be painted like I see it, there would be no kick coming from me. When folks like the things Ma Nature has made and don't want man's improvements, this is a good place for them."

This section of the country was peopled by many kinds of wild things. We saw deer almost every day. Charlie put salt out for them, and we could watch them from the cabin window. They were not afraid to bring their young with them for they were confident nothing would harm them.

A covey of mountain grouse lived in the brush nearby, with huckleberries, service berries and wild rose hips for them to feed upon, and they were not bothered by men. An old mother Loon and her twins fed along the shore. Charlie liked their strange, lonely screams. And he liked, too, the sound of the owl calling to its mate after dark. That sound would have made some folks lonesome—not Charlie. He was happy hearing the language of wild things. He loved all the outdoors west of the Mississippi. But the loneliness of a big city overwhelmed him. Crowds of human beings made him feel crushed, suffocated. He wanted a clear view; he wanted to take a deep breath of air that had not already been breathed by others.

One of his favorite tricks was to put a chicken bone in a tomato can, then push the cut part in so that the bone would be too hard to get at. He then placed the can where we could, from our window, watch Mr. Skunk try frantically to get that chicken bone out. He worked for that bone, but with little success.

Sometimes we walked with our picnic lunch back through the trails to Bubble Spring, a queer [i.e., odd] place where the water came up from a blue clay bottom in silver bubbles as large as a tea-cup to break at the surface, spreading the rings across to each bank, more following until there would be three or

WE SAW DEER ALMOST EVERY DAY. CHARLIE PUT SALT OUT FOR
THEM, AND WE COULD WATCH THEM FROM THE CABIN WINDOW.
THEY WERE NOT AFRAID TO BRING THEIR YOUNG WITH THEM
FOR THEY WERE CONFIDENT NOTHING WOULD HARM THEM.

Deer at Lake McDonald (1908), Charles M. Russell.
PETRIE COLLECTION.

Charlie painted several versions of this scene at Lake McDonald. Despite his earlier
modest denials, his depiction of lake water in this 1908 image was much more than
pretty good!

more on their way at one time. There must have been some kind of medicine about the place that bear[s] liked or needed, as there were usually fresh signs. One day the grass and logs were still wet where Mr. Bruin had just gone out.

We visited, too, the beaver meadow about three miles from the cabin. Here we saw the superb engineering of the wise old beaver who had directed the building of the dam that protected his home.

As we walked through the trails, Charlie never missed anything that grew: the lichens on the trees or toad stools grouped like Chinese villages, spider webs gleaming in the sun or tall trees asway in the wind. Sometimes we watched a big soft cloud roll up over the garden wall, saw the rain shower sweep down the lake to quiet its surface. And when the sun had broken through, a rainbow would span the lake, a crowning glory to the great outdoors . . . . .

ONE DAY THE GRASS AND LOGS WERE STILL WET WHERE MR. BRUIN HAD JUST GONE OUT.

Nancy's reference here is to an undoubtedly exciting "near" bear encounter close to Bull Head Lodge itself. This watercolor was inspired on another such occasion in Glacier Park, as recounted by Isabel Russell, Charlie's niece and the daughter of his brother, Bent Russell: *"This scene, with Lincoln Peak [Glacier Park] in the background, was painted August 19, 1910. Charley Russell, his wife, Nancy, and a party of eight were camping nearby. After the party had set up tents and eaten, they went for a twilight stroll. Suddenly, a rustling and clambering was heard. Two grizzlys appeared closeby. Fortunately, the wind was blowing toward the human party and the bears did not notice them.*

Charley painted the scene the same evening. The following day, he presented it to his niece Isabel Russell (later Wenneis) for her birthday."

As continues to be the case today, exciting bear sightings were not uncommon in Glacier Park.

Two Grizzly Bears (1910), Charles M. Russell.
COLLECTION OF TERI L. AND BRUCE R. BROCK.

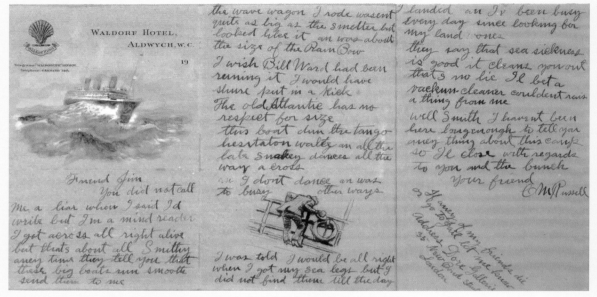

Letter to James R. Smith ("Friend Jim"), March 30, 1914, Charles M. Russell.
PETRIE COLLECTION.

Charlie's letter to his businessman friend, James R. Smith, back in Great Falls provides an amusing and detailed account of Charlie and Nancy's acute seasickness while
crossing the Atlantic Ocean. It is the first of a dozen Russell illustrated letters from that
trip that provided much of our direct knowledge of the couple's experiences, prior to
the appearance of this manuscript by Nancy.

London
[1914]

In Canada [at the first Calgary Stampede in 1912 as well as a year later in Winnipeg] we received so much encouragement to show Charlie's work in London that we began to think seriously of such a plan. As we were going to New York that winter with the pictures for exhibition, I started immediately to lay the foundation for an exhibition in London [in April 1914]. Arrangements were made with the Doré Gallery in Bond Street. [Today these are the auctioneer offices of Sotheby's.]

My first thrill came in sending a cable and getting a reply dated before the original message had left me! After our exhibition in New York we arranged to bond the pictures so that they would get into England and out again without trouble.

———

We crossed on the Oceanic, which later went down during the [First] World War. Strangely enough, the same fate was met by the ship we chose for the return voyage—the Lusitania.

March is a very bad month on the Atlantic, and the ocean did everything but empty us out of the ship. And two prairie people were very sick! Charlie said, "I feel like I swallowed a bull snake, and he won't keep still." There was someone in the next stateroom who was also very sea-sick. Charlie called out, "Wait a minute; I'll throw in with you!"

The poor, suffering man on the other side of the wall would then be quiet for a while.

We continued to be so ill ourselves that with what strength we had left we decided to get off at Plymouth. And for the first time in our married lives, Charlie had to pack up the bags. To my surprise he did a very good job.

It was wonderful to get onto the ground, except that it was less solid than we had supposed it would be, for it had a swell like the ocean and kept us from walking [in a] straight [line] for over a week after we got to London.

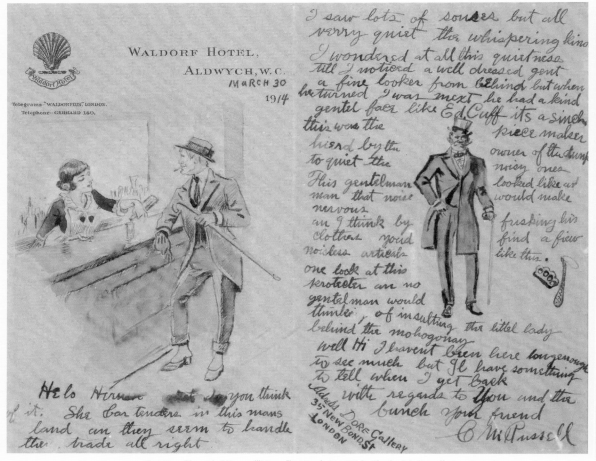

Letter to Keros A. Hinote ("Hiram"), March 30, 1914, Charles M. Russell.
PETRIE COLLECTION.

Complementing Nancy's account of British perceptions of American women and their custom of chewing gum is Charlie's bemused report to one of his bar owner friends in Great Falls on English drinking traditions and the bouncer's influence over inebriated patrons in the presence of a female bartender. Such an arrangement stood in sharp contrast to that in Montana where the Silver Dollar and Mint Bars were closed to regular male customers on certain days in order to be "suitable" establishments for ladies to come and enjoy seeing Russell's art.

We got through customs miraculously in no time at all and entered the boat train for London. Charlie's first thought was for a substantial breakfast, and we at once found the diner, where I had the first food I had eaten since leaving New York—except for a saltine cracker and a split bottle of champagne. Charlie liked the English bacon and sole and grilled tomatoes.

So our visit to England began auspiciously.

We were amazed by the neatness of the woods we passed through. There was not a twig on the ground, and there were no waste papers or boxes or cans to be seen anywhere. At the stations beautiful little flower gardens smiled at us.

At the London station the trainman said, "You must look after your own luggage."

That was some assignment! We couldn't run in so many directions at once after the various pieces of luggage. But finally we got them all together and got a man to take them.

We stayed at a small hotel where the doorman was most kind in directing us to the gallery at Bond Street. When the bus conductor asked for the fare, Charlie held out a handful of silver so strange to us with these words, "Take it out of that." The addition of sixpence assured us that we would not go past our corner. With the greatest politeness we were told which way to turn to get to our destination.

The boxes of pictures had been delivered to the gallery, and the manager was anxious that they should be hung as soon as possible. So that was the next thing to be done—to get the exhibition in order.

When the pictures were in place, a great banner was swung out over Bond Street, announcing "Charles M. Russell, cowboy painter of the West that has passed."

And often later, as we rode along the bus, we would see sandwich men telling [their customers] about the exhibition.

At 4 o'clock every afternoon all of us quit work and went into the main office of the gallery for tea. Then the men would smoke, and as I didn't smoke, the attendants regretted that they did not have some chewing gum to offer me! I assured them that I didn't care about chewing gum.

"Oh, don't all American women chew gum?" they asked, baffled.

"Not all of them," I said, "and not all of the time."

It was an education to meet the art critics in London. They did not want to be introduced to either Charlie or me until after their criticisms had been written. They didn't want our personalities to influence them in their judgement.

But the results couldn't have been any better if we had tried to tell them how good we were. The English people like outdoor action pictures. Most of them are great travelers and have seen a good deal of life, so when it is put on a canvas that is true to life, they appreciate it. So Charlie's work was received with marked enthusiasm and understanding.

Once the favorable criticisms had reached the press, there was an excellent attendance at the exhibition. It was interesting to see an elderly man with a group of young boys taking pleasure in the collection, asking such natural questions about the handling of horses and cattle.

Although it was April and the World War [WWI] was but four months away, we heard no whisper of trouble on the continent. So different was it from the months preceding the present war [Note: Nancy is contrasting it with the onset in1940 of WWII]. Occasionally we heard talk of the trouble with Ireland, but the opinion seemed to be that it would be straightened out in no time. So people were happy and gay; the exhibition continued to be well attended; and we made friends and were invited to English homes— which we understood was the thing that never happened!

However, Charlie had so much that he was doing for the world that the English accepted him as a man who had done his part [by informing the public about western American history] for coming generations. They recognized his genius and were not slow to say so.

One of the people who came to see the exhibition was Sir William Ramsay. He had heard of Charlie through his brother-in-law who lived in Montana. He and Lady Ramsay invited us to dinner at their home near Regent's Park.

When we rang the doorbell, a tall, liveried servant appeared. We both felt that we should bow to him, he looked so impressive! He took our wraps, then showed us the way upstairs where the party was waiting. The door was opened; we were announced, only to find ourselves decidedly bewildered in this strange drawing-room. We gradually drifted to the end of the room where most of the guests were assembled. I think I was enticed over there by the sight of cups of steaming tea in the hand of the guests. Not accustomed to the utter lack of heat in English private homes, I had innocently come clad in a whisper of chiffon dress because it was becoming! However, my chattering teeth didn't add to the charms of the gown, and nothing ever seemed so welcome as that first cup of hot tea. I was pleased to see how eagerly Charlie juggled his cup, too; I suspected that he was just as cold as I, in spite of having several more layers of clothing.

Almost immediately dinner was announced. I went with Sir William, and Charlie escorted Lady Ramsay. When they reached the threshold of the dining-room, Charlie naturally stepped back to allow Lady Ramsay to enter the room first. But in stepping back, he landed on her train, and there was a harsh, ominous sound of ripping silk. The gown seemed to be crying out in horror that its wearer was going to be minus a train in a minute.

Lady Ramsay hesitated, seemed to be about to kneel. My cowboy husband straightened the train so that his hostess could proceed without further mishap.

Charlie later confessed that he had suffered with embarrassment the entire evening and wanted desperately to ask someone how a lady could go through a doorway without having her escort step on her gown. Long after we had got back home, Charlie had forgotten his embarrassment enough to tell his cowboy friends about his little difficulty. But they were of no help to him, for they could suggest nothing more skillful than [what] he had done.

At any rate, Charlie was sure that Lady Ramsay would never forget him.

A man we had met in Canada, Mr. Hamilton Pfyfe of the Daily Mail, looked Charlie up in London and wanted to show us some interesting places in England. He took us out along the Thames River to Windsor Castle. In the nearby park were many deer, the sight of which delighted Charlie. All of it was as nature had made it, and the animals were happy.

Mr. Pfyfe also took us to the little church about which Gray's Elegy was written, and we visited the spot where Gray and his mother were entombed. I am sure the same tree stood near the church where lived the owl that Gray immortalized in his Elegy.

This was one of many happy excursions to see the country and its treasures. Stratford-on-Avon was not more interesting to Charlie than that day spent on the Thames.

At Broadway, where lived artists of all types, Charlie visited the home of Millett [Francis Millet] and there saw the work of Elma-Tadema [Lawrence Alma-Tadema]. These men were great friends, and there were many examples of their finest work.

HE TOOK US OUT ALONG THE THAMES RIVER TO
WINDSOR CASTLE. IN THE NEARBY PARK WERE MANY DEER,
THE SIGHT OF WHICH DELIGHTED CHARLIE.

detail from *Royal Cortege at Windsor Park* (n.d.). Engraving by F. Bromley of original painting by R.B. Davis,
detail created by Luc Demers.
PETRIE COLLECTION.

[During our visits to galleries and museums] Charlie loved the smaller pictures of artists; for instance, he especially enjoyed the Wallace collection in London because of the small picture of Mesange [a type of bird].

At Broadway Charlie also had tea with Mary Anderson Navarro, the famous American actress. I missed this treat because I [Nancy] was out climbing through hedges in the search for wild hyacinths. A game-keeper came along just as I untangled myself from one hedge. In great surprise he asked, "Did you come through there?" And when I nodded in reply he said, "It will be easier to go through the gate down below. It's a quarter of a mile away." I objected that the gates were all locked, but he assured me that this one was not. [One interpretation of this is that he may have been discreetly and politely telling Nancy where she would not be trespassing!]

At any rate, the troublesome hedges were responsible for keeping me from the tea-party. But in addition to rents in my clothes and scratches on my skin, I had a lovely bunch of wild hyacinths. They made up, in small measure, for the lost opportunity of taking tea with the glamorous Mary Anderson.

Because England was natural and was the mother of all the countries Charlie knew, he loved it. Everything was old and settled, and this appealed to him, too. However, he was continually struck by the fact that—as he put it—there seemed to be more people under the ground than on top of that island.

The Scout (1915), Charles M. Russell.
PETRIE COLLECTION.

Joshing Moon (1918), Charles M. Russell.
PETRIE COLLECTION.

The Scottish artist John Young-Hunter met Charlie and Nancy at their Dore Gallery exhibition and they quickly became good friends. He then accompanied the Russells to Broadway in the Cotswolds. He may also have arranged their tour of the Wallace Collection at Hertford House in London. Nancy's observation about Charlie's interest in smaller pictures is interesting in that he produced several exceptionally fine smaller works of his own over the next few years after returning from London. Above are two examples of his masterpieces in relative miniature: *The Scout* (1915), measuring 16 x 21 inches, and *Joshing Moon* (1918), measuring $8^1/_2$ x $13^1/_2$ inches.

In the case of *Joshing Moon* Charlie composed a poem, "Christmas in the Foothills (Joshing Moon)," to accompany the painting as a Christmas gift for Nancy. While Charlie was not accomplished in terms of formal schooling, his ability to communicate verbally became increasingly powerful as the years unfolded. In part, these skills seem to have developed in conjunction with his deepening friendship with and appreciation of, among others, Irvin S. Cobb and Will Rogers.

* * * * * * * *

Christmas in the Foothills (Joshing Moon)

That joshing moon a-riding skies

Has got me looking through kid's eyes

Tonight, if I'd heard them jingling bells

And pop of lash like maw once tells

I'd bet this is old Santy's team, all right;

But if it 'tis, he's shy a line hoss now.

The lead bull's in my pan, I'll bet a cow

For when this old gun busts a shell

It's meat for Christmas, sure as . . .

Well, it won't be canned nor slicings of a sow.

I been out all day and never seen a track;

Looked like there'd be no Christmas at my shack,

But my luck knocking down this bull

Will bring me more than both socks full

As free as outa Santy Claus's pack.

—Charles M. Russell

EVERYTHING WAS OLD AND SETTLED, AND THIS APPEALED TO HIM, TOO.

Nancy's closing comments for this section about how "old and settled" appealed to Charlie are interesting considering that when they visited the Tower of London, Charlie was rather amused to learn that someone bearing the Russell name had been interred (and possibly executed) there centuries earlier. Perhaps this helps explain why over the next few years following their return home, Charlie did several watercolors and even composed verses demonstrating how taken he had become with tales from English folklore. Below are examples of these deviations from his typical western subjects. I am particularly impressed with his ability to capture the feel of ancient English oaks that are so evocative of those around my wife's cottage in southern England. [T.A.P.]

Knight and Jester (1917), Charles M. Russell.
PETRIE COLLECTION.

Knight and Friar Tuck (1917), Charles M. Russell.
PETRIE COLLECTION.

The verse in lower left of the picture of *Knight and Friar Tuck* reads:

> Thy gown doth not belie thy faith,
> Thou hath a saintly way,
> If blest are those who cheerfully give,
> Art thou not blest this day.

(As was often the case, the calligraphy here was done by Russell's friend Josephine Trigg.)

Friar Tuck (bronze cast from the plaster model), Charles M. Russell.
PETRIE COLLECTION.

Pursuing further the "Friar Tuck" theme, Russell fashioned a model in honor of that legendary figure.

* * * * * * * *

My Gift

My gift is gold of kingdom's make
'Tis trash for misers made
Which mortals love and robbers take
By might and length of blade
Thy song is much the greater gift
Thou hast the power to send
For music is the gift of God
To throat or a finger's end.
—Charles M. Russell

* * * * * * * *

I Drink Not to Kings

I drink not to king in castle strong
With fighting men at call
Who boasts behind his armored throng
That lay within his wall,
But fear to leave their draw bridge gates
In numbers or alone
Without their blades and armor plates
They're but a stingless drone.

I drink to thee, a giggling clown,
With garments well befit.
Thy smile is armor for the frown,
No weapon but thy wit.
Thou goest alone and weaponless
Where armed men fear to trod
For steel and blade are devil made
But wit's a gift of God.
—Charles M. Russell

Paris
[1914]

M R . M I L L E R H A D F I N I S H E D H I S W O R K in London and was going to Paris to buy pictures for the [Osborne] calendar company of which he was president. He thought Charlie should go to see the pictures there, too. Charlie had a contract with the calendar company for a certain number of pictures a year. Mr. Miller was convinced that Charlie should go to Paris for the purpose of learning the number of artists producing pictures to be sold for calendars. [Russell had just contracted with the Osborne Company to provide pictures for their art calendars prior to sailing from New York.]

Of course, any woman so close to Paris would want to go there to see the latest fashions. Very anxious to go, I was delighted to have an unconscious conspirator like Mr. Miller. It took a good deal of argument to convince Charlie that he must forget he was a western cowboy and see what was being done in the supposed center of the civilized world. Mr. Miller won by announcing that he had the tickets and we were to leave the next day, when he would call for us at the hotel.

I left England much more gaily [happier] than Charlie because I was doing something I had secretly wanted very much to do. But Charlie was going against his will every inch of the way. And when he didn't want to do a thing, he never did get over not wanting to do it.

From the moment he set foot in Paris, he was uncomfortable. He was ashamed to come to a country where he did not speak a word of the language. Of course, he blamed only himself, but that did not make it any easier. He said he had trouble with their French, but not nearly so much as they had with his! The only thing he consented to do was to visit the galleries. I wanted to go up the Eiffel tower—and never did I get there! I wanted to walk through the woods of Fontainebleau where walked Marie Antoinette. And never did I see that! Charlie said, "You can be satisfied with looking at the fancy cut of the Frenchman's whiskers." He called them bearded ladies, because their greatest accomplishment seemed to be the designing of women's clothes.

At the Continental Hotel we met [the Moronis,] a couple from the West. Charlie knew the man very well so was delighted to see him. He asked them if they knew any place where he could get some hot bread—biscuits, muffins or pancakes. Mrs. Moroni replied that she knew a place where we could get corn meal cakes with ham for breakfast.

Charlie said gratefully, "If you take me to get something like that here, when you come back to Great Falls I'll cook you the best hot breakfast you ever tasted." Which he could and did do—much later.

Mrs. Moroni, who was getting a new wardrobe, invited me to go with her to see the models. I enjoyed it very much until I realized that I was the center of whispered conversation. I could see amused glances directed my way, and when I moved in front of a large mirror, I knew what it was all about. It was a rainy day, and to save my only good suit I was wearing a wool dress with an English cravanette storm coat—a good-looking enough coat, but not at all the thing to wear to a place like that, especially with a lady who was dressed like a peacock. The sales people couldn't understand when Mrs. Moroni said, "Show my friend such-and-such a model." They looked deliberately beyond her as if to see whom she was speaking of. They didn't think it could possibly be I [me], for they thought I had got in quite by accident with my raincoat and little green suede hat. I have never liked green suede since then! I saw many beautiful models and Mrs. Moroni gave her order for a wonderful wardrobe. I managed to swallow the lump in my throat until I got back to the hotel. [In my essay on page 94 of the catalog for *Charles M. Russell: The Women In His Life and Art*, I liken this incident of scorn to a very similar scene of disdain in the movie *Pretty Woman*. (T.A.P.)]

Then I rushed to my room, and as I passed the bathroom I reached in to get a bath towel that was as big as a bed blanket. Then the tears broke loose. I had never been made fun of before (that I knew of!), and at the moment it was more than I could take. Although I didn't howl, the water dripped, and right in the midst of this demonstration Charlie and Mr. Miller came to the room to say that it was time to go out to dinner. Charlie exclaimed, "What's the matter with you? I thought you were so happy to be in Paris!" Then, "Wa-ait a minute! Put on your rubbers before you get your feet wet."

But sympathy only made matters worse, and I wept until Mr. Miller

Thackeray Hotel, London England

May 6th 1914

Friend John here wer are in old old England the grand Dad of civilization an I wish you were here to look at your GrandPa

Letter to John Matheson, May 6, 1914, Charles M. Russell.
COURTESY JOHN R. HOWARD FINE ART, MISSOULA, MONTANA.

Charlie did not enjoy the side trip to Paris, but he observed something there that he knew would interest his old friend, the retired freighter Johnny Matheson, who inspired paintings like *The Jerk Line* (p. 30) with his twelve-horse team pulling loads up dauntingly steep inclines. The French, Russell said, *"string there teames like the sketch Im sending an handel them with a jerk line."* They used huge horses, and while he saw *"a great many"* teams there were *"never more than four horses but as each hors wayed about the same as 3 cyuses it was equel to a twelve hors team an would drage about the same weight."* This is the only letter known to show and describe something Charlie saw on his short stay in France.

sternly said, "Go wash your face and powder your nose and stop this fool-ishness. We're going to dinner."

To which Charlie added, "Yes, hurry up, because if we don't have him to order for us, we'll starve!"

Charlie wanted strength, too, for the next day, when he had promised to go with me (as he put it) through thirty-five miles of hats to find a little Paris bonnet. We got the hat, and I was so proud of it and felt well-dressed in it for years, as it was different from anything I could ever see anywhere else. I never met myself coming from another direction.

Mr. Moroni once asked Charlie, "You don't like Paris, do you?"

"No, I don't."

"You would like Rome," said Mr. Moroni. "You would see so many things there that you would enjoy. You should go down to Rome."

Charlie's whole heart was in his voice as he answered, "No! There's only one place on earth I want to see—and that's home!"

So we left Paris to go back to England for a few weeks more before we sailed away for America and home . . . .

I'D RATHER GO INTO THE RING WITH JACK DEMPSEY THAN [RIDE] SOME HORSES I KNOW.

Charles M. Russell and Jack Dempsey (1923), photographer unknown.
MONTANA HISTORICAL SOCIETY RESEARCH CENTER, HELENA, MONTANA, PHOTO ARCHIVES (944-787).

Charlie's preference for getting "into the ring" with Jack Dempsey versus riding some horses he knew reflected personal experience. A longtime boxing fan, in 1923 he attended the Dempsey vs. Tommy Gibbons fight held in Shelby, Montana, having personally met Dempsey while he was in Great Falls training for the bout. As Nancy relates on page 118, Charlie also had a firsthand adventure being thrown off one of Con Price's so-called reformed bucking horses.

Following the Dempsey vs. Gibbons fight, Charlie modeled (in plaster) the boxers. It was posthumously cast in bronze, as shown here.

The Boxers (ca 1922-23), attributed to Charles M. Russell
by Joe De Yong and cast by James Cagney May 5, 1971.
PETRIE COLLECTION.

Contest Riders

*[Nancy cobbled this chapter together from letters Charlie wrote
that were not used in* Good Medicine.*]*

I NEVER THOUGHT I'd have to go hundreds of miles to see a bronc ridden. In old days, the puncher who rode a string of snakes [bucking horses] had his shirt tail out most of the time. [Charlie to Johnnie Mullens, April 18, 1925] I'd rather go into the ring with Jack Dempsey than [ride] some horses I know. Jack would put me to sleep, the horse would unload me, but with Jack [I] wouldn't fall so far. It's a long way to the end of a MacCarty going up, but you've noticed it's a dam sight further coming down. You come faster and there is no chance to rough lock.

"Years ago a horse sent me up on the Yellowstone, and I saw the Sweet Grass Hills. Some of the boys asked me if I went up after my hat.

"I would sure like to see the contest in the South. The only cow punchers I see these days are in the movies or at a contest. The Old West is wired now—but I'm glad we still have broncs and bronc riders. My hat's off to all riders and ropers. They are all we've got left of the Old West. They are real men, and I'm glad I know some of them. Will James [Charlie wrote on December 26, 1924], you never got you're material from photographs, you got it with a horse under you and sometimes you couldn't keep him there. [See commentary on page 150.]

"You've smelled the smoke of dally and felt the jerk of a tye. You've handled the rope when it wasn't used for a clothes line. I'm glad you are turning out books. There'll always be cows, but they will be hornless and broke to lead they won't need cowboys to rope them. Rattle a bucket and they'll come. This kind will stay anywhere they can smell a silo. The cow you know will go but there will always be people that like to see pictures and read about cows with horns and real men that handled them. [Charlie to Will James, ca. January 1926:] Maybe man-made beef makes good steaks but they don't make stories or pictures. The horned cow may be crowded off the earth by man-made deformities but those with horns will live always in books and pictures. James, you could not have written a book like yours [*The Drifting Cowboy*] about hornless cows. If you did nobody'd read it but the butchers."

JAMES, YOU COULD NOT HAVE WRITTEN A BOOK LIKE
YOURS [*THE DRIFTING COWBOY*] ABOUT HORNLESS COWS.

I Was Handed Some Mighty Tough Ones (1929), Will James.
PETE LEIDEL COLLECTION.

Nancy is highlighting Charlie Russell's regard for Will James' riding skills with tough horses. This painting suggests why that is the case.

Will James was a larger-than-life figure with both a name change from Ernest Dufault and a largely reinvented (fictitious?) past. His level of fame as a writer and artist in the 1920s in some ways approached that of Charlie Russell. Depending on who you believe, he first met Russell in either 1912 or sometime between 1917 and 1920. In between those periods he served jail time, as he admitted, for cattle theft. While their first meeting was disappointing for James, Charlie's view of his success with self-illustrated books (ultimately totaling twenty-three) was more respectful, as Nancy's quote suggests. She, however, was more reserved, perhaps due to the wider popularity of James' books versus the first editions of the *Rawhide Rawlins* volumes. Overall and notwithstanding his publishing success, James earned a mixed reputation for reliability, as Larry Len Peterson describes in *Charles M. Russell: Photographing the Legend* and as Harold Von Schmidt has also observed.

Saskatoon
[1919]

FOLLOWING THE VICTORY STAMPEDE in Calgary in 1919, at the college one of the big halls was scheduled for a special exhibition of the Russell work for the young Prince of Wales. We knew the date that he was expected to be in the city, and in due time we were notified by the mayor of the hour that the prince would come to see the pictures. We learned, too, that he had requested Charlie and me to be there.

An amusing thing happened. The people of the city had got their very best clothes especially pressed and ready to wear for this exciting occasion in the city's history. But a telegram from the young man spoiled all their plans, for he announced that he would be wearing a lounge suit and a Fedora hat—so that caused all the high hats to go lie down and wait for another time [for their best outfits] to be taken out and dusted and worn!

At the appointed time the party arrived at the gallery. The attendant opened the door leading down the steps into the gallery. The prince came first, ten or twelve steps ahead of the rest of his party, which was composed of a number of much older men. We assumed that they were the advisers who found the young blood a bit hard to control.

The prince came directly to Charlie and me, and we advanced to meet him. We did not know just what was expected of us in greeting, so we simply walked forward and held out our hands, American fashion, and he grasped ours with his left hand, saying, "My people loved me so much in Toronto, they put my right hand in the hospital." And indeed, it was in a sling.

He was a fine example of a young man of whom any nation would be proud. Slight and very active and interested in all the new things in this new country.

He immediately started looking with great attention at the Indian pictures and said, "Mr. Russell, they are representatives of a long time ago, are they not?"

There was one thing you should know of this young fellow: he was so entirely human and so anxious to live a normal life. He was a guest at the

"MR. RUSSELL, THEY ARE REPRESENTATIVES OF A LONG TIME AGO, ARE THEY NOT?"

Edward, Prince of Wales, with Ray Knight, Alberta rancher, Russell patron, and manager of the special Saskatoon Stampede, taken shortly before the prince inspected Russell's exhibition at the University of Saskatchewan, September 11, 1919, photographer unknown.
BRIAN W. DIPPIE COLLECTION, VICTORIA, BC.

Whiskey Smugglers Caught with the Goods (1913), Charles M. Russell.
COURTESY OF THE WILLIAM I. KOCH COLLECTION.

This painting of the North-West Mounted Police was one of the Canadian subjects in the Russell exhibition viewed by the prince in Saskatoon.

Bar-U Ranch where he wanted to ride horseback and requested a good horse of the owner. Mr. Lane, the owner [and one of the four co-founders of the Calgary Stampede], told his foreman, "Give him a good horse but a gentle one; we're not going to kill any [future] king around here!" Some of the horses were, in fact, outlaws and would kill a man.

The second morning of his visit at the Bar-U, the Prince of Wales awakened early and went out the window and down to the river. When someone came to awaken him for breakfast, he wasn't there, and great alarm swept the place. No one had seen him. But when he finally appeared, he said, "It was such a fine morning—I had to take a walk."

But his visit will probably be best remembered by the wife of one of the bigwigs of the town who was completely horrified to learn that we had shaken hands with His Royal Highness instead of saluting him in manner befitting his station. She did not realize that he was too big a man to make anyone uncomfortable because of the wrong greeting.

The woman counselled me strongly against washing my hands, and she even held my hand so that she could know my clasp as the prince had.

Inscription by Nancy Russell and William S. Hart in *My Life East and West* by William S. Hart,
AS PRESENTED TO FORD E. ROSE (BOSTON: HOUGHTON MIFFLIN COMPANY, 1929)

Bill Hart and Nancy remained close friends for the rest of her life. After his autobiography was published, Nancy sent a copy of it to Ford E. Rose inscribed and autographed by both Hart and her. Indicative of their special friendship, the inscriptions read:

Transcript:

Ford E. Rose on his Birthday with all the good wishes for the future from Nancy C. Russell an old friend of Bill Harts.

Dear Ford E. Rose—

I am saying happy birthday, too: only I'm not a friend of Nancy Russell—I love her—first loved her as she wore pigtails down her back—and always will until the final curtain falls—

This goes for the great man thats gone on ahead making trail—also—/ Meta Kola [Your Friend, in Lakota] /

Bill Hart

Bill Hart Writes a Letter

Jan. 22, 1929

Dear Nancy:

It's a great task to try and set down my memory of Charlie Russell, one of the greatest men that ever pulled on a pair of cowhide boots.

As you know I first met Charlie at your home in Great Falls, Montana, the early part of January 1902. You were in the next room listening to the actor's talk, you were too bashful to come in. I was playing John Storm in The Christian at the time and great Falls was a one night stand. After the performance Charlie was heard to remark—"The feller that didn't do no talking in the day time [W.S. Hart] was the star of the show at night."

I knew many illustrators and painters in New York and the impression Charlie made upon me was so great that I begged him to make a trip East. I think it was during the following winter at my little flat on West 34th Street, I received a card bearing a New York postmark, reading, "Friend Bill:

How! I'm in the big camp."

There was no address given, just Charlie's emblem, the buffalo skull. It took me several hours to find him, but I did. He and your good self were living at a little hotel (The Park) on 42nd Street near Sixth Avenue [today the site of the New York Public Library].

I was out of an engagement during those days and Charlie and you and I spent much of our time at the studios of Will Crawford and J. N. Marchand, also on 42nd Street. None of the artists had any money, but they were making a living. [In 1903 and '04] I was plumb broke and I have always thought the Russell family were doggone near the bottom of the pocketbook too.

Do you remember, Nancy, how we would all congregate at the studio of Crawford, Marchand, Walter Galloway, Fred Yohn, Ed Ash, or one of the many others of the artist crowd, and have a party meal on the share and share alike plan? Yes, and draw lots to see who would wash and wipe the dishes. I remember one night when I was wiper [heard a gunshot and] I dropped a plate and you women folks all screamed and the men folks all rushed for the windows [to see the noise that distracted me]. Hell was poppin' down below on 42nd street, seemed

THE ONE DIFFERENCE BEING THAT IN THE "OLD TIMES"
WITH SUCH A FUSILLADE OF BULLETS THERE
WOULD HAVE BEEN SOME CASUALTIES.

The Gun Fighters (1904), Charles M. Russell.
JOINT COLLECTION OF TOM PETRIE AND THE C.M. RUSSELL MUSEUM (TD2018.9.1).

While neither Nancy nor Hart mention it, construction of the new building for the New York Public Library was underway right next door to the Park Hotel where they were staying and the adjacent building housing John Marchand's studio. In fact, as this project progressed for over a decade, both the hotel and studio structure were ultimately demolished, most probably to accommodate the library's full footprint. One is left to wonder if the Monk Eastman shooting incident that Charlie, Hart, and friends likened to the old "wild and wooly" Montana West actually stemmed from a labor dispute on this gigantic construction project.

In any case, when Charlie returned to Montana after the first trip to New York, he seems to have been inspired to paint *The Gun Fighters* (aka *Death of a Gambler*). Implicitly it stands as a statement about the accuracy of "straight shooting" western gunmen with whom he was personally familiar.

like more shots were bein' fired that had been in the Spanish-American war, also there was the sound of running feet and breaking glass. "Seems like old times," said Charlie. And it was. The one difference being that in the "old times" with such a fusillade of bullets there would have been SOME casualties. But the next morning when Charlie was looking at the bullet holes in the big plate glass windows along the street, he remarked, "Them fellers sure must have been shootin' at tall men." "Looks like the wild and wooly west, doesn't it, Charlie?" someone said. "It's wild all right, but not very accurate," replied Charlie. Monk Eastman and his East side gang of gun boys did not measure up.

I had no money. Thru a relative I secured some trip passes on the Long Island Railroad—you an Charlie and I used to journey to the most lonesome part of the ocean. Golly! How Charlie loved it. When the great body of water was lashed and tossed by the elements, I will never forget the picture he made, his body bulging with muscular strength, his leonine head uncovered, his tawny blond hair whipping in the wind, his outstretched hands saluting the waves with the tenderness of a child. He seemed the reincarnation of some giant norseman of the early ages.

As you will remember, Nancy, Charlie had never seen the sea until those days, nor had he ever been aboard of a sailing ship. How I chuckle when I think of a few days later—when the captain of one of these greyhound specimens of ocean craft nearly kidnapped Charlie and would have done so I think had you and I not been along. The burly master of that full rigged sailing beauty that was bound around the horn for Australia surely wanted Charlie for a shipmate. The sailor of the sea knew the sailor of the plains.

And then the trips to my little 34th Street flat and the boiled beef and horse-radish that my darling mother used to cook.

Gosh, Nancy! Do you remember the first picture you sold? It was three hundred dollars [of increased price] and Charlie insisted you should have it all. You bought a fur coat and based on the recollection of those dancing blue eyes and ecstatic little yelps, I'll gamble my last nickel that, after twenty-six years, you know where that fur coat is hanging right now! Such coats clothe our bodies but they warm our hearts with a heat that never dies.

The last time Charlie and you and I met was shortly before Charlie took the long trail. We seldom talked of the old days. It seemed that for some years we had sort of grown away from them, but this day we all went back to the old

YOU BOUGHT A FUR COAT AND BASED ON THE
RECOLLECTION OF THOSE DANCING BLUE EYES AND
ECSTATIC LITTLE YELPS, I'LL GAMBLE MY LAST NICKEL
THAT, AFTER TWENTY-SIX YEARS, YOU KNOW
WHERE THAT FUR COAT IS HANGING RIGHT NOW!

Nancy Russell's fur stole.
C.M. Russell Museum, Great Falls, Montana,
GIFT OF JANE AND TOM PETRIE (2012.1.1).

Nancy C. Russell, December 1921.
Photograph by Roland Reed, Denver, Colorado.
COURTESY BRIAN W. DIPPIE COLLECTION, VICTORIA, BC.

This fur throw of Nancy's is likely a modified (cut down) successor to the fur coat Hart
is referring to in his letter to Nancy. I also strongly believe that this sales transaction
is the one Nancy describes on page 107. While she recalls the price was $400 and
Hart's recollection was $300, I suspect that Hart was remembering the approximate
difference between Nancy's price versus the $100 or so that Hart and Charlie were
contemplating when her boldness overrode them. Thus, Charlie gave her the $300
uptick to spend on the fur. [T.A.P.]

days—and when I went away—there was rekindled in our hearts hundreds and hundreds of thoughts that were—oh! so dear! And then a little while later Charlie WENT AWAY—and I said a little prayer and I know that God hear[d] it on account of the man it was about.

 All good be with you, dear Nancy.

 Your friend,

 Bill Hart

William S. Hart and Charlie Russell on the set of one of Hart's Westerns, photographer unknown.
GILCREASE MUSEUM, TULSA, OKLAHOMA (TU2009.39.275.7).

Story Teller

MANY'S THE TIME when we have been in a crowd, someone would say, "Tell us a story, Mr. Russell!"

That was usually fatal. Charlie could no more tell stories to order that he could paint flowers. If people [left] him alone, he would drift naturally into his storehouse of yarns; especially if some guest would start telling his experiences, Charlie would find himself following up with a story of his own. Before he realized it, he'd have the floor and could talk for hours, never telling the same story twice, [and] never laughing at his own jokes. But one could see that marvelous light of humor in his eyes and the play of muscles and lines in his face, showing how deeply he enjoyed making others laugh.

Once he had started talking, a friend could say, "Oh, tell us the cheese story," or request some other favorite which he had heard Charlie tell. And Charlie could go on telling the stories they asked for, never seeming to tire.

His ability to read people came from being a thoroughbred himself. He had a perfect insight into human nature. As a rule, men liked a different working for a story than could be used in mixed company. Charlie told the tale their way, but he could without hesitation tell the same story in a drawing-room filled with the most fastidious women—and none was ever offended.

That favorite cheese story went something like this:

In the Spring of 1889, Charlie went back to the Judith to his old job of wrangling. The captain was Horace Brewster, the same man who hired him in 1882 on Ross Fork.

Some of the boys came into Philbrook to celebrate. While they were at the post-office and general store, the postmaster told them someone had sent him a piece of limburger cheese through the mail. He didn't know what to do with it, as he wasn't acquainted with anyone "civilized" enough to eat it. So he gave it to the punchers, who put in a lot of their time rubbing it on door knobs, the inside of hat-bands, and on drinking cups.

They had the whole community smelled up in pretty good shape, when someone discovered an old timer [named Bill] who had come into town to spend his "roll" [pay] and become unconscious from the "joy juice" he had imbibed. His heavy, drooping moustache gave one of the punchers a brilliant idea. A council was held, and it was agreed that he should have his share of the cheese rubbed into the moustache under his nose. Being unconscious, Old Bill slept as innocently as a babe while the work was done.

Next day Charlie saw him out back of the saloon, seated on a box, looking mighty dejected. He would put his hands over his mouth, breathe into them, then drop them in a very helpless sort of way.

Knowing full well what had happened to Bill the night before, Charlie went over to him and asked, "How are you stackin' up today?"

The old fellow looked at him with tragic eyes and shook his head. "Me? I'm not so good."

Charlies asked, "What's the matter? Are you sick?"

"No-o-o, not more than usual. I've felt as bad as this a thousand times, but—!"

Then he covered his face again with his hands. After a few seconds he slowly lowered them, shaking his head and groaning, "Oh, it's something awful. I don't savvy."

Charlie, all sympathy, said, "What seems to be the matter Bill?"

"Damned if I know, but I've got the awfullest breath on me. 'Pears like I'm plum spilt inside. You can tell the boys my stay here on earth is damn short. Nobody could live long with the kind of a breath I got on me. Oh! Oh!"

Then he would breathe into his hands again, murmuring, "Oh, Gawd!"

He would have been sick sure enough if they hadn't told him the truth.

Story Teller #2

Tom Clarey, a fine man, owned a freight outfit. He had nine wagons (three teams) and eleven yoke of bulls to the team. There was one man to each team and night herder to hold the cattle. Tom didn't drive a team, for he was the boss.

The outfit was on its way to Lewistown. One of his bull-whackers had just quit, and he had hired the first man he could find at Fort Benton, where they camped that night. The new fellow was to take a team the next morning. When supper was ready, each man took his tin plate and cup, went to the dutch oven to get his grub, then found himself a place on the ground to sit and eat it.

Tom's first discovery about the new bullwhacker was that he ate with a fork. Tom decided that was too high-toned a way for a bullwhacker to eat, so he fired him without giving him a chance to drive.

A few years later Tom met that fellow he fired. Looking at him rather strangely, Tom asked, "Do you know why I fired you?"

The other answered, "Well, I heard it was because I ate with a fork!"

"Ye-e-s," said Tom ruefully, "Mary (Mrs. McClary) makes me do that now."

Joe Kipp

AT AN INDIAN CELEBRATION in Browning, Montana, Charlie was a guest of the Blackfeet who had one skin lodge left from the old days. The greatest compliment they could pay him and his white friend was to have it set up for their use.

Their personal host was one of the head men, Joe Kipp by name, a mixed blood who was a fine story teller with a good memory. Charlie asked him why he didn't write about his country, the people and customs he knew.

"Ye-s-s, I do that, and the white men would hang me, you know."

Charlie and Kipp were in the general store [Kipp's Trading Post] for some Bull Durham for Charlie, who rolled his own cigarettes. He bought a five-cent sack of tobacco, and as he turned away, a blanketed Indian stepped up [to] the counter.

"I take same kind tobacco. How much?"

To Charlie's amazement, the clerk replies, "Ten cents."

The Indian paid it, made the sign "good smoke" and walked out.

Joe Kipp made the Indian sign "not good" and "talks with two tongues."

Then he said, "Now you see, my friend, why I don't write about my people."

The Robe Trader (1898), Charles M. Russell.
Courtesy of the Buffalo Bill Center of the West, Cody, Wyoming;
WHITNEY WESTERN ART MUSEUM (1.85).

The Petition

THE MOTHER OF A YOUNG MAN who had been convicted of working over a brand and was serving a term in the penitentiary came to Great Falls to see if she could get her boy pardoned. She asked Bob Ford, an old timer who had turned banker, if he would help her.

Old Bob said, "Yes, I'll do my best."

He asked Charlie to take the petition around. Everyone Charlie called on signed it, with the exception of one man—another banker—who refused, saying, "That fellow can spend his life in jail before I'll sign it. He is a crook and should pay for it. I'm surprised at you, Charlie, for trying to get a man like that pardoned. As far as I'm concerned, I'll never sign anything."

Charlie had his suspicions about a man who thinks he is too good to give the other fellow the benefit of the doubt, but he said, "If you don't want to sign it, all right—but don't roast me. He was my friend. While I admit he might have done wrong, there may be others among us, if we had our just dues, who would be there with him, making horse hair bridles [in jail]."

True enough, this hard-hearted gentleman banker was later indicted and found guilty of [mis-]using other people's money. He was sentenced to serve a term in the same prison.

John Mathewson,
Jerk Line Man

JOHN MATHEWSON [MATHESON] had the last jerk line team in Montana; three wagons, twenty horses ten span he drove with a jerk line— that is, [all on] one line connected with the leaders.

When civilization pressed Charlie too hard, he took his tooth brush and started off for a visit with John, who was a bachelor and very shy of women. Charlie did the cooking, which pleased both of them.

I remember Charlie's telling about one special trip:

"Barring a bad snow storm, we had a fine trip. We were snowed in so we didn't turn a wheel for three days, but we were comfortable.

"John slept in his cook cart, and I in the trail wagon, and there's no better snoozing place than a big Murphy wagon with the roar of the storm on the sheets. Nature rocked my cradle and sung me to sleep."

John ran his freight team from Ft. McGinnis [Maginnis] to Big Sandy. He and his partner had to ferry their team across. The ferry was operated by a wooden pulley on a cable stretched across the river. When John and his partner misjudged the angle of the boat, it swung 'round in the current—nose down-stream—and they couldn't pull it at all. It was stuck in the middle of the river!

In such a situation Johnnie lost his temper almost to the point of insanity. He pranced back and forth on the old ferry boat, threw his hat down and stamped on it.

And when there was an unexplained crash at the back of the wagon, his rage knew no bounds, and the air was blue with his cursing. He demanded to know what his partner had done now. The man replied that he had done nothing, but the grub box had fallen off of itself.

"What should I do with it?" he asked.

Johnnie roared, "Throw the damn thing in the river!"

The partner—cool and deliberate fellow who took others at their word— picked up the whole outfit and threw it in the river.

Johnnie, seeing it disappear, stormed, "My God, man, don't you know you've thrown away our cooking outfit and grub?"

"I can't help it, John, you told me to do it," calmly answered his partner.

It is a difficult thing to turn a corner with three wagons and twenty horses, to get a big enough swing to keep all the wagons on the road. One time in Lewistown a wagon bogged down in the mud. The team could not move it.

John's calm again deserted him, and he was talking a bit wildly to the horses when a very fat woman came up and said, "You should be ashamed of yourself, talking like that to those poor horses."

Now John's anger was too much for him. He just looked at her a second, then said, "Lady, if I had you on the wheel, we'd pull out of here without a word."

[“My Charlie Sais”:
Poetic Reflections]

[Perhaps appropriately, Nancy's unfinished manuscript ended with several poems written by Charlie. Those directly referencing Russell works of art have been relocated close to the pertinent images (“His Heart Sleeps,” page 108; “Christmas in the Foothills (Joshing Moon),” page 141; “My Gift” and “I Drink Not to Kings,” page 143. Others, however, provide general insights into Russell's take on life. Nancy printed one as her Christmas greeting in 1929 following the words “My Charlie sais.” Consequently, it leads off her selection of five poems, all untitled, about the deeper meaning of gifts and good wishes.]

* * * * * * * *

A gift may look small and worthless
Though if wrapped with love and tied
Then it's the wrapping that has value
Not the money-bought thing inside

* * * * * * * *

‘Tis not from tomb of Rameses
No priceless jeweled thing
Nor was it ever treasured
By some ancient mummied king.
With clay, wire and paint
I done the best I could
My fingers give in sentiment
More than diamonds would.

* * * * * * * *

Good wishes is a broke man's gift,
But if my wish comes true
You'll get all that's good, my friend,
And I've gone broke on you.

* * * * * * * *

Here's hoping your trails a long one
Plain and easy to ride
May your dry camps be few
And health ride with you
To the pass on the Big Divide.

Here's Hoping the Worst End of Your Trail is Behind You (1926), Charles M. Russell.
C.M. RUSSELL MUSEUM, GREAT FALLS, MONTANA (953-1-021). GIFT OF THE JOSEPHINE TRIGG ESTATE.

* * * * * * * *

Behold a soldier of fiction
Who's just as unreal as he looks.
Like romance and myth, who he travels with,
He only lives in books.
Some say he's not needed and useless,
Though he's loved by age and youth.
We know it's true there's only a few
That really do love the truth.
Of course we find truth in the papers,
With murder and death by the hour,
But a lie that is flavored with romance
Is sweeter than truth that is sour.
The truth gives us castles and rivers
And perhaps merry England's green wood.
But we know 'twas not truth but romance
That gave us the bold Robin Hood.
The truth gave us Christmas and stockings,
But you know well, you maws and paws,
'twasn't truth but old lady myth
That gave us the good Santy Claus.

Charlie and Nancy at home in Great Falls (1926), Branson G. Stevenson.
MONTANA HISTORICAL SOCIETY RESEARCH CENTER, HELENA, MONTANA, PHOTO ARCHIVES (944-685).

Nancy and Charlie Russell, by their back gate at home in Great Falls in 1926, the year they celebrated their thirtieth anniversary, a month and a half before Charlie died.

Coda

[NANCY CONCLUDED her "Life of Charles M. Russell, Artist" with Charlie's own loving and honest appraisal of their relationship:]

This lady I trotted in double harness with was the best booster and partner a man ever had. She could convince anybody that I was the greatest artist in the world, and that makes a fellow work hard. You can't disappoint a person like that, so I did my best work for her.

She had a very quick, hot temper and had not learned to control it like I had. I had learned to control mine, so when differences came up I would take my hat and go down town, and when I came back the clouds would have all passed away. I would come in the back gate happy and whistling, and she would meet me with a smile. She would be so sorry for her misdoings.

Birthday greeting for Lewis O. Evans, August 30, 1926, Charles M. Russell.
PETRIE COLLECTION.

Russell's sentiment was universal: Wouldn't we all prefer to become younger each year, especially as our years seem to pass increasingly quickly?

Afterword: Trail's End
by Thomas A. Petrie

IN THE SUMMER OF 1926, following goiter surgery at the Mayo Clinic in Rochester, Minnesota, Charles M. Russell was informed that he did not have long to live. He returned to Great Falls in July and then went on to Bull Head Lodge. At an August 30th birthday party for Lewis O. Evans, the owner of Kootenai Lodge at nearby Swan Lake just south of Glacier Park, he once again demonstrated his command of touchingly succinct English in a handcrafted birch bark card he prepared for Evans:

Russell's sentiment was universal: *Wouldn't we all prefer to become younger each year, especially as our years seem to pass increasingly quickly?*

Charlie's passing occurred only seven weeks later, in October 1926, and was not unexpected. His surgery at the Mayo Clinic had been successful but had also revealed serious deterioration of his cardiovascular system. His poor health undoubtedly gave rise to thoughts about mortality and how he wanted to be remembered. In December 1925, he had written his own eulogy in a remarkable foreword to *More Rawhides*, "A Few Words About Myself."

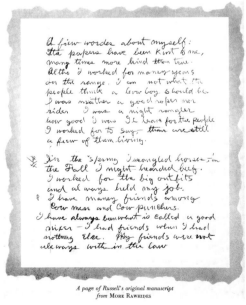

*A page of Russell's original manuscript
from* MORE RAWHIDES

A Few Words About Myself, Charles M. Russell,
AS PUBLISHED IN *RAWHIDE RAWLINS*, TRAIL'S END PUBLISHING (1946), FIRST REVISED EDITION.

A Few Words About Myself:

THE PAPERS have been kind to me,—many times more kind than true. Although I worked for many years on the range. I am not what the people think a cowboy should be. I was neither a good roper nor rider. I was a night wrangler. How good I was, I'll leave it for the people I worked for to say—there are still a few of them living. In the spring I wrangled horses—In the fall I herded beef. I worked for the big outfits and always held my job.

I have many friends among cowmen and cowpunchers. I have always been what is called a good mixer—I had friends when I had nothing else. My friends were not always within the law, but I haven't said how law-abiding I was myself. I haven't been too bad nor too good to get along with.

Life has never been too serious with me—I lived to play and I'm playing yet. Laughs and good judgment have saved me many a black eye but I don't laugh at other's tears. I was a wild young man but age has made me gentle. I drank, but never alone and when I drank it was no secret. I am still friendly with drinking men.

My friends are mixed—preachers, priests and sinners. I belong to no church, but am friendly toward and respect all of them. I have always liked horses and since I was eight years old have always owned a few.

I am old-fashioned and peculiar in my dress. I am eccentric (that is a polite way of saying, you're crazy). I believe in luck and have had lots of it.

To have talent is no credit to its owner for what man can't help, he should get neither credit nor blame—it's not his fault. I am an illustrator. There are lots better ones, but some worse. Any man that can make a living doing what he likes is lucky, and I'm that. Any time I cash in now, I win.

—CHARLES M. RUSSELL
Great Falls, Montana

A Few Words About Myself, Charles M. Russell, as published in *Rawhide Rawlins* (1925).

Russell's horse-drawn hearse (1926), photographer unknown.
C.M. RUSSELL MUSEUM, GREAT FALLS, MONTANA (X990.8.44).

In her memoir, Nancy chose to include an untitled poem by Will Aiken that had appeared in the press with an introductory note, as follows:

"In accordance with the request of Charles M. Russell, the hearse which [conveyed] the body of the 'cowboy artist' to its final resting place was drawn by horses. For that occasion, Will Aiken of Helena, Montana, penned the following poem:"

Not the muffled purr of the car's exhaust,
 Nor the faintest grind of gear.
Nor yet the speed of our hurrying day
 shall 'tend the cortege here,
But the steeds of flesh and blood he chose,
 Not spent and flecked with foam,
With measured hoofbeat, soft and low,
 Shall bear the artist home.

From that long-gone day when the goddess Fame
 alone knew when and where
She would turn her flaming wand on him
 Who then stood silent there.
He had loved his horse, yes, every horse,
 Through noonday sun, through gloam—
So now the horse with measured tread
 shall bear the artist home.

The brush has fall'n from lifeless hand,
 The colors soon are dry,

Not ever again shall Russell's charm
 gild plain and hill and sky.
But we know his love for his old range friend
 was staunch as heaven's dome
As we see the steeds with measured tread
 As they bear our loved one home.

With Russell's passing there soon began and continues to the present day an active market in memorabilia that honor his memory, his friendships, and his artistic legacy. For example, in 1926 Charles O. Middleton, a Los Angeles-based art dealer, inscribed as a Christmas gift to Frank Tenney Johnson and his wife Vinnie a signed copy of Russell's *Rawhide Rawlins Stories* that reads:

It is a pleasure to have you as friends. It's a pleasure to have you near us at Christmas time. It's a privilege to be able to express my appreciation with something that I know you will value as highly as you will this copy of Charlie's western tales.

When I wrote him (while he was very ill) that the books you wanted for Christmas greetings, he took the trouble to autograph them — one of the very last things that he did before he was called by the great Boss.

Some six years later during the Great Depression, a number of well-heeled art collectors and special Russell friends gathered on March 19 to honor his memory on his birthday.

This event is evidence of the early success of Nancy's mission after she became a widow to deepen the public appreciation for the artistic legacy of Charles Marion Russell. Considering the prominence of his works in many of today's museums and leading auctions of Western American Art, many would agree that she resoundingly achieved her goals. Furthermore, this occasion became the first of many examples of collectors gathering on March 19 to celebrate their appreciation of the C.M. Russell artistic legacy.

Final Thoughts
by Brian W. Dippie

NANCY RUSSELL'S BIOGRAPHICAL MEMOIR came about because she realized that Charlie Russell's death on October 24, 1926, did not have to mean an end to interest in his life and work. She had negotiated with Doubleday in New York to publish an illustrated collection of his short stories, *Trails Plowed Under*, which debuted to critical acclaim within a year of his passing. The book complemented Nancy's desire to keep his name before the public since she planned to make her living after he died the same way she had while he was alive, promoting and selling his art to those enamored of his romantic vision of the Old West. As she told the contractor who was building a new home for her in Pasadena, "I feel, with the clientele I have, I should be able to make enough for Jack [their ten-year old son] and me to live on and I will be busy with the thing I know best." When Nancy and Jack left Great Falls and moved to California less than two months after Charlie's death, she was already thinking about a new book project featuring his art. An illustrated biography had been suggested and Nancy hired Dan Conway, an unemployed Great Falls newspaperman, to churn out a manuscript over the summer of 1927. It was finished and submitted to the publisher of *Trails Plowed Under* that October, and rejected as unpublishable a month later.

Still, the idea swirled around in Nancy's head. Perhaps she could write the biography herself—in effect, a biographical memoir. If she recycled portions of Conway's manuscript in her book, so be it. She had paid for it, after all, and its title page read: "A Child of the Frontier: Memories of Charles M. Russell (The Cowboy Artist)" by Dan Conway, "Written under the direction of and in co-operation with Nancy C. Russell." Or would the publisher, who had rejected Conway's manuscript, prefer an entirely different book, a collection of Charlie's illustrated letters showcasing his sense of humor, his wisdom, and his wizardry with a pen? The publisher opted for the letters book, and while Nancy continued to work on a Russell biography, her focus was on completing *Good Medicine: The Illustrated Letters of Charles M. Russell*. Brilliantly conceived and produced, it suffered from unfortunate timing, appearing just months after the stock market crashed

The History of the West Studies (ca 1925), Charles M. Russell.
COURTESY TREVOR REES-JONES COLLECTION, DALLAS, TEXAS.

In summarizing the rising prices she had obtained for Charlie's art, Nancy concluded with the most lucrative payday of his career: $30,000 from California oil man Edward L. Doheny for a mural in two panels, measuring 2½ feet high and 43 feet long in total, called *The History of the West*. Charlie completed it in the spring of 1926, just months before he died. For Nancy, who had negotiated the commission from start to finish, it represented the pinnacle of her success as Charlie's business manager and she was justifiably proud of her achievement.

Shown above are the four watercolor studies that Charlie prepared for Doheny's approval. (This book's endpaper illustrations are matching details from the finished mural.)

in October, 1929. Though the book did well enough, nothing could prevent the erosion of the art market during the Great Depression. In her biographical memoir, Nancy intended to trace the arc of Charlie's story as she envisioned it. For her, success was the tonic, and it would be her theme, measured by the escalating prices she secured for Russell art. None of the notes she jotted down as prompts to her memory, setting the agenda for her book, is more revealing than a single page charting the rising prices she had obtained, and Charlie's dazed reaction:

Dead man's price--15.00 1900--$400.00 for a picture in N.Y. 1903 near fainted--10,000.00 in Las A. [Los Angeles] 1919 Dead man's price--30,000 1926 Cant read it [too many zeros]--

Nancy's record of ever-rising prices came to an abrupt end in the Depression years. When she died in 1940, an oil painting she had valued at $30,000 was appraised by one incompetent Los Angeles art dealer at $250—about half of what a Russell painting had commanded in New York in 1903 when his prices were just beginning their meteoric rise and Nancy had to mop her husband's brow to keep him from fainting.

If success proved fickle, Nancy had other memories to fall back on in telling the story of Charles M. Russell. Her biographical memoir would have included them had she enjoyed good health in the later 1930s and finished what she had begun. We know this from the notes she left behind, defining the full scope of her projected memoir. She even completed some of the tasks she set out in them, including chapters on the Russells' trip to London and Paris in 1914 and to Saskatoon, Saskatchewan, in 1919, where they met the future king of England. Her notes, mementos of Nancy's ambitions for her book and a guide to where she meant to go, provide the perfect note on which to conclude her unfinished adventure "Back-tracking in Memory."

ROSS HOLE FOR BACKGROUND OF
LEWIS & CLARK PAINTING

Lewis and Clark Meeting Indians at Ross' Hole (1912), Charles M. Russell.
MONTANA CAPITOL, COURTESY MONTANA HISTORICAL SOCIETY, HELENA, MT (X1912.06.01).

In a letter dated November 14, 1936 to an engineer with the Montana Highway Commission, Nancy explained the setting for "the Lewis and Clark painting which is back of the Speaker's Desk in the Capitol":

"Charlie and I went up to Ross-Hole where he sketched the background. We stayed at Darby and hired a buckboard to take us around through that part of the country so that Charlie could get the lay of the land where the expedition is supposed to have met the Flathead Indians. . . . Charlie purposely used the meeting in Rose-Hole because it was on Montana soil . . .*"

Ross' Hole site visited by Charlie and Nancy as it appears today.
PHOTOGRAPH BY THOMAS A. PETRIE WITH SPECIAL THANKS TO MY GUIDE, DOUG NELSON.

*Montana Historical Society Archives, Helena

Appendix

NANCY'S NOTES: Prompts for what Nancy intended to cover in her biographical memoir, in the Charles M. Russell Research Collection (Britzman), Gilcrease Museum, Tulsa, Oklahoma. My transcriptions follow Nancy's entries as best I can decipher them, with a few passages grouped to accommodate the sequence she apparently intended. Like Charlie, Nancy was a freethinker when it came to spelling, and I've silently corrected most of her mistakes for clarity's sake, retaining just a few for flavor. [B.W.D.]

———

Notebook One [Dec. 2, 1928-Mar. 26, 1929] (E. 309)

Ideas I have not worked out—

Chas as a Bull whacker—

stealing the honey from Bumble bees nests—

A good shot at a [fine squirrel?] when the bunch were in the mts [mountains] with old [hoover?]— [The sentence is hard to read, but may refer to an incident during Charlie's time in the Judith Mountains with hunter and mentor Jake Hoover]

Ross Hole for back ground of Lewis & Clark painting The [vegetation and?] boy that drove the team—[The Russells in 1911 hired a wagon and driver to visit the setting for his State Capitol mural, *Lewis and Clark Meeting the Indians at Ross' Hole* (1912)]

I brought you this bottle of Bourbon

Thank you Bill [Bill Rance, proprietor of the Silver Dollar Saloon in Great Falls] we will use it for mince pie as Doc cut the tank out of me [Charlie stopped drinking hard liquor after his appendix was removed in 1907]

If both hands were cut off I could learn to paint with my toes it is not in my hands but heart what I want to paint. (an Injun sais)

I wish you could see the things I see—

I'll never have time to paint all the thing[s] I dream

his work came out of the store house of the beauty that formed his character

I cant do all I know I wont have time—

If I lived a thousand years I couldnt do all I know—

he could pick beautiful exquisite thing[s] out of the dirt of life—all men were honest [last sentence crossed out]

[In a separate note (C.8.321) Nancy expanded on her thoughts:

Mrs Lewis [wife of John Lewis, owner of the Lake McDonald Hotel and Charlie's hunting companion] sais the first thing Chas did when he hit the mts [mountains] on their yearly hunts was to find some kind of a little feather and stick it in his hat and it was his medicine—

Chas was always so sensitive to beauty—the family were amused by the things he said and did when he was a cute looking tow head in those days he seemed to feel every one noticed his brother Eds golden curls altho the two boys were almost like twins— . . . [See the first chapter for the family story that followed]

Describe Oak Hill in detail well, wine house, Negroes cabins drive way flower beds Kitchen living room, fire places [Presumably a request put to Sue Portis, Charlie's older sister and Nancy's primary source for information about his childhood]

Branding calves at Eskers [?] out of Cascade [1895]

"Lollie Edgar" [Laura Edgar, Charlie's first sweetheart, a St. Louis girl who summered in Montana in the early 1880s and spent one full year there before returning to St. Louis in 1885]

Chas as a Bull whacker

never gambled—Had a saloon 16 days at Chinook

Tried to build a cabin on a squatter claim

would rather cook a meal than turn the water on the garden

—smoked opeum [presumably Charlie tried opium once!]

Rolling down the hill in a barrel there was one boy with long curly hair and when this barrel started his long hair was flopping in mid air as he bounced around in the rolling barrel the minute every boy landed and could stand up and see[,] the other boys would wink at him and then would say Gee that was fine I want to go again in that way every boy did it once but that was enough—

One time Chas was visiting his cousin Fergus Mead in the city Their house had a lovely curved stair way at the back for the servants . . . This was just fine for a toboggan so the boys [took out Ma's?] lap board all that could crowd on did and down they came and when the bottom was reached the lap board was splintered and all the grown up[s] in the house were out in the back yard so Chas said they thought the roof had fallen in from the noise they heard or an earth-

[An earthquake, presumably; the anecdote ended mid-word, and while Nancy relished such tales of Charlie's boyhood antics, she trimmed back on them in her final draft to keep the focus on "Charles M. Russell, Artist"]

————

Handwritten note (C.11.2):

Trip to Mexico [1906]

The time we could not go to the Circus [Adam Forepaugh & Sells Bros. Circus created a sensation when it toured Montana in early August 1896; Nancy was actually thinking of the Ringling Brothers Circus, which played Great Falls the next year]

When we took Jack after our trip the [to] Arazona [1916]

When we moved to Great Falls, [1897]

Fathers [Charles Silas Russell's] visit, when we built our home with Mothers [Mary Mead Russell's] Legacy [1900]—first trip Lake McDonald—then building Studio in Great Falls, [1903] and lake cabin [Bull Head Lodge] at McDonald [1905-06]

Red Bird [Charlie's horse] had to be killed. [1900]

Charles S. Russell on a visit with Charlie and Nancy in Montana (ca 1898), photographer unknown.
PHOTOGRAPH COURTESY OF BUDD RICE, BRIAN W. DIPPIE COLLECTION, VICTORIA, BC.

Handwritten note (C.13.49):

From a Bull fighter to the future King of England

Lummis [Charles F. Lummis] Author, explorer

Birth Lynn Mass. March 1st 1859

Harvard class /88

walked Cin [Cincinnati] to La [Los Angeles]

3,507 miles 143 [days required]

5 year with S.W. Indians - founder S.W. Museum and Land markers.

house [El Alisal, which Lummis built himself] Birth day party - dress

bull-fight Mexica Fuenta "Blood & Sand

Placecard from C.M. Russell's 60th birthday celebration, March 19, 1924, Charles M. Russell.
PETRIE COLLECTION.

Beginning in 1920 the Russells wintered in Southern California where they formed new friendships and cemented old ones. Nancy intended to write about some of them in line with a talk she gave in Great Falls in 1921 about *"interesting people I have met."* Charlie's sixtieth birthday party was a case in point. It was held on March 19, 1924, at the W. C. Tyler residence in Los Angeles where the Russells and Joe De Yong were staying. Harry Carey and his wife Olive, both silent screen Western movie stars, picked Charlie up in the afternoon and took him to the circus then dinner to keep him occupied until the birthday guests had all arrived. Thirty-one people, including the Tylers, Russells, and De Yong, attended the party, and Will Rogers, acting as master of ceremonies, regaled them with jokes and stories until the party broke up around 2 a.m. De Yong reported, *"He gets $1,000.00 per performance as an after dinner speaker so at that rate the bunch here got about $10,000 worth of wit and humor for nothing."*

Charlie had prepared individual place cards for the guests, each with a unique western figure. The card shown above was done for Will Rogers. On the reverse side are the signatures of all the attendees, including Charlie and Nancy, Will and Betty Rogers, Charles F. Lummis, Harry and Olive Carey, Ed Borein, Gene Stratton-Porter, and other notables. Charlie, being Charlie, also invited ordinary folks, including old friends from Great Falls and Nancy's half sister, Ella Ironside.

Charles F. Lummis, Charlie and Nancy, and Harold Lloyd, Los Angeles (1922), photographer unknown.
GILCREASE MUSEUM, TULSA, OKLAHOMA (TU2009.39.5657).

Hanky

Lummis Wife translator—Four [books by Lummis? Children by his second wife?]

Medal from King of Spain—

Bill Rodgers [Will Rogers]

home

Goldwyn studio—Pershing—

Mary Pickford

Douglas Fairbanks

Lunching

Newspaper clipping: "Famous Artist and Movie Star Photographed Together" (1924).
GILCREASE MUSEUM, TULSA, OKLAHOMA (TU2009.39.5592).

Seeing first shot of "The Three Musketeers"

Notables who have been to galleries to see [Russell] pictures

Richard Mellon

house

Irving Cobb

his letter—

Answer—

Visit to MacKays [Malcolm and Helen Mackay, whose home in Tenafly, New Jersey, boasted a rustic "Russell Room" devoted to Malcolm's collection of Russell art]

Millets home at Broadway [Francis and Lily Millet's home, Russell House, center of an artist's colony in Broadway, visited by Charlie and Nancy while in England, 1914]

Sargent [John Singer Sargent]

Abbey [Edwin Austin Abbey]

Alma-Tadema [Lawrence Alma-Tadema]

Mary Anderson-Navarro [American-born actress]

Southwark & Marlow [presumably William Marlow, born in Southwark, London]

John Alexander [John White Alexander, a New York artist]

Mural painting [White reassured Charlie that he was up to tackling the mural for the Montana State Capitol in 1912]

1912 at Calgary [Stampede]

Royal party [the Duke and Duchess of Connaught, and their daughter Princess Patricia]

1919 Sept. Saskatoon

Prince of Wales

Typed note (E 68):
Miscellaneous Notes

Mr. Russell says, "An arrow being carried in quiver lay point down and naturally signifies peace."

"Grown folks like stories told in picture. I'm one of that species of grownups." —Mr. Russell.

Charlie's horse fell with him and sprained his right wrist so badly that it was in a cast for six weeks, starting the early part of July 1919 at which time he was painting a picture for the Duke of Connaught [*When a Left Handshake Is the Safest*] to take to the Calgary Stampede.

When a Left Handshake Is the Safest (1919), Charles M. Russell.
ROYAL COLLECTION TRUST / © HER MAJESTY QUEEN ELIZABETH II 2019 (RCIN 407538).

Charlie had an exhibition of pictures at the Minnesota State Fair Sept. 1920; from there they went to the Milwaukee Art Institute.

Exhibited at: Brown Palace in Denver in Dec. 1921.

Corcoran Art galleries, Washington, D. C. Spring of 1925.

Look up De Hart's correspondence in inactive "D" folder. [Jake L. DeHart was Montana's State Game and Fish warden in 1919, when the legislature proposed to abolish the department, inspiring an illustrated letter from Russell that became a popular poster promoting game conservation, *The Hunter's Crime*]

In Denver, during the time of our show at the Brown Palace, 1921, there was a smallpox scare and all the trains from Kansas City, were being fumigated and watched [washed]. Charlie and I were vaccinated for smallpox in Denver It is a very funny thing-- we went to call on some very wealthy people who we hoped to sell a picture to. During the evening, their physician came to vaccinate the lady for smallpox, as the scare had reached Denver. They thought it would be fine to be vaccinated at the same time, so we went one at a time with the physician to the lady's bathroom and were vaccinated. Chas. had been vaccinated when a boy, so it did not take with him. It sure took well for me!

November 26, 1921, we went to Brown Palace for Denver exhibition.

We spent the winter of 1919 and 20 at 866 N. Chester Ave., Pasadena.

The winter of 1923 spent at 509 E Cabrillo Blvd., Santa Barbara.

"I agree with you as to the cowpuncher boot. The cow puncher in my time took great pride in his boots and hat. He generally came from a brand of small feet and hands and wore a tight and light boot. This was the old-time cowpuncher. They may not be like that. Here's good luck to you. Stay on the wagon. I've been riding it the past seventeen years and I'm feeling better every day. It's the first part of the road that is the hardest."—Russell. May 19, 1921.

"The Spirit of the Buffalo"—The Indians believe all animals live again in another world and as the buffalo meant 'life', to them his robe housed and clothes him, his flesh was food, so when smoking, [t]he Indian often prayed to the buffalo, holding his pipe to the skull and asking that his kind might always be plenty.

"The West owes much to men of [Jim] Bridger's breed. All wild men were not red-skinned,—long-ranged guns were often the white man's passport."—

Titles of pictures—"The White Man's Buffalo" -(cow)

A Mother's Claim" - (cow claiming her calf)

When Guns Were Their Passports (ca 1924), Charles M. Russell.
GILCREASE MUSEUM, TULSA, OKLAHOMA (01.912).

Handwritten note [1936] (E 61):

Beating the soles of a drunks feet to bring him to

calf branding at Cascade 1895—

Twisted papers between the drunk mans toes-

Fires at Lake [McDonald]—1924 & 26—Judge [James W.] Bollinger

Mince pie at Cascade—

sawing wood with a cross cut saw in the wind-

adopting Jack—[1916]

Biltmore Gallery—(the picture is not worth it—) 1926 Dead Mans price—

15.00 1900—

$400.00 for a picture in N.Y. 1903—(near fainted—

10,000.00—in Las A. [Los Angeles] Dead mans price 1919—

30,000 1926

Motion Picture star Tom Mix was looking at pictures—

liked one very much said dont you think that is good[,] Russell[?]

Ah ges [guess] but I can do better-

120 original water colors on hotel menus—for $20.00 Park Hotel [in Great Falls] 1899 [actually 1897]

Raffled a 6 ft picture for which Chas received 105.00 a banker won it on one $1.00 ticket sold it three years later to an other banker—for 5,000.00—

A $15.00 picture sold for $7500.00 made an elderly couple comfy for life including a trip to the Old country—

Charles M. Russell, Nancy C. Russell and Jack Russell (1918), photographer unknown.
GILCREASE MUSEUM, TULSA, OKLAHOMA (TU2009.39.273.56).

Maroney [Maroni] in Paris—want to go to Rome—Hot cakes & ham—lonely for his people and Co. [country] buying hats for me—Taxi driver—Art galleries—

buying clothes with Mrs Marony in [Paris] manikins [mannequins] [sales staff] laughing at my English out fit—Chas & Mr Miller find me in tears—[1914]

Lecture with President Taft met him in Helena [1909, presumably, when President William Howard Taft spoke at the opening of the Montana State Fair; Taft was presented with a Russell watercolor, *Roping a Grizzly* (1903), at a breakfast banquet in Butte two years later]

Pres Harding met Chas in Butte stopped the parade to talk about one of his models Best Rider Quit—[The first cast of the bronze *Where the Best of Riders Quit* was presented to President Warren G. Harding by the Shriners in Butte, 1923]

President Harding meets Charlie Russell, Famous Cowboy Artist, Butte, Montana (1923),
KEYSTONE VIEW COMPANY OF MEADVILLE, PENNSYLVANIA. BRIAN W. DIPPIE COLLECTION, VICTORIA, BC.

Special exhibition [at the 1912 Calgary Stampede] for Duke & Duchess of [Connaught] Princess Pat [Patricia, their daughter]

Saskatoon show [1919] and the Prince of Wales now Geo VIII [actually Edward VIII; the "now" dates this note to 1936]

Corcoran Galleries Washington Sen. Walsh [Thomas J. Walsh, of Montana; 1925]

London show in Bond street 1914—

strangers that were taken in by the Eng [English]

Brangerson [?] Studio-

[John] Young Hunter a friend

English critics

Late to tea

Sea sick

Our visit to the Church around which Grays Elegy was written. - Cold meat pie for supper—Our Visit to Paris with Miller of Osborne Cal [Calendar] Co.

first one man show in N.Y. [Folsom Galleries, 1911] Arthur Hoeber getting a page in the N Y Times

Meeting Bill Crawford & [John N.] Marchand in Mont

Their influence in getting Chas to N Y- from the St Louis Fair

Being broke and borrowing money to go Eat

the double N Y [Arthur H. Harlow] and Corcoran at Wash [1925]

Ed Newlon—Block in Lincoln Nebraska—R.R. tickets & turtle soup—

Mexico 1906—Arazona 1916—

Charlie and Nancy Russell on the road to the Cortez Sugar Mill, Mexico (1906), photographer unknown. From a photograph album of the Russells' trip to Mexico.
C.M. RUSSELL MUSEUM, GREAT FALLS, MONTANA (T990.740).

Acknowledgments
by Thomas A. Petrie

MY DELIGHT IN HAVING Brian Dippie's fully engaged collaboration is expressed in my Introduction. Here, I reiterate and emphasize that this would not be the book it is without him

Janeen Hogan, my executive assistant of some thirty-seven years, played a critical role starting from the project's most initial phase to its final stage. Her judgment, advice, and eagle-eyed attention to detail gave me confidence that I was staying consistently on track. In addition, I would like to acknowledge my partners at Petrie Partners, who have generously granted me considerable flexibility and support while I focused on this biography. Several of our firm's analysts and other employees were especially helpful during the assemblage of digital images in this work. Those include Dwight Clark, Jackson Kinsley, and Morgan Morris. Denver-based photographer Mike Jenson was instrumental in providing high-resolution images. Further away but critical to this project, Chuck Rankin, formerly the editor-in-chief of University of Oklahoma Press and now retired in Helena, Montana, was especially helpful when I "got stuck" for a time while working on my introduction. His editorial talent that served Janeen and me so well when publishing *Following Oil* proved similarly valuable in this case. His timely advice about collaborating with Brian Dippie has made all the difference, which he wisely foresaw.

Brian and I are both indebted to a number of individuals whom we wish to acknowledge for their input and support while we developed this project. Susan Neal, executive director of the Gilcrease Museum, quickly facilitated access to the Britzman archival material, which was essential to filling in certain blanks in Nancy's typescript manuscript. Gilcrease's generous permissions regarding images from its extraordinary collection of Russell works was an important addition to this book. Numerous other professionals, friends, and dedicated Russell collectors and institutions had a way of showing up just when needed to help address various issues that arose on our path to publishing Nancy's personal story of what ultimately became the C.M. Russell art enterprise with her at Charlie's side as wife and business partner: Thomas Brent Smith, executive director of the Denver Art Museum's Petrie

Institute of Western American Art; Byron Price, director of the Russell Center at the University of Oklahoma; Karen McWhorter, Scarlett Curator of Western Art at Buffalo Bill Center of the West; Sarah Boehme, Curator Stark Museum of Art; and Jim Peterson, recent past chairman of the C.M. Russell Museum Board of Directors.

From the beginning of our collaboration both Brian and I envisioned this book to be a publication of the Frederic G. and Ginger K. Renner Research Center at the C.M. Russell Museum. Accordingly, we have been gratified (even elated) to have received the enthusiastic backing of the C.M. Russell Museum's board, management, and staff. This includes its executive director, Thomas Figarelle, and senior staff members Duane Braaten, Justin Campos, and Brenda Kornick, as well as Kathryn Kramer. Kathryn's attention to the multiple details of assembling correct credits and permission has been exemplary.

As the full manuscript came together, we greatly appreciated the C.M. Russell Museum's current board chair Larry Len Peterson's introduction to Farcountry Press/Sweetgrass Books, based on his many book publishing ventures with them. With his beneficial suggestions regarding cover design and other details, Larry kept us focused and encouraged throughout the publishing process. It has been a team effort to fashion Nancy C. Russell's initial manuscript into a published book. We are especially grateful that Kathy Springmeyer at Farcountry Press and her very capable successor, Erin Turner, quickly identified both the merits and challenges of this project. Their commitment ensured that Nancy's voice prevailed, enhanced and amplified by the additions of Charlie's images and our editorial commentary. The result was a reinforcement of our vision of what Nancy's decade-plus writing endeavor could ultimately become. Jess LaGreca's creativity in designing the layout linking images and Nancy's text confirmed our belief in the importance of presenting and sharing Nancy's unique perspective on "Charles M. Russell, Artist." Trevor Rees-Jones as well as Rick and Murfy Stewart deserve special thanks for enabling inclusion of Russell's mural images as endpapers to this book.

Finally, we deeply value the courtesies provided for publication of images extended by many owners of Russell-related art and other materials. All are identified where their art appears in the text, and their generosity in accommodating our permission requests was key to presenting to readers today Nancy Russell's account of "Back-Tracking in Memory."

Sources Cited

Foxley, William C. *Frontier Spirit: Catalog of the Collection of The Museum of Western Art* (Denver, CO: The Museum of Western Art, 1983), 99.

McCullough, David *Mornings on Horseback: The Story of An Extraordinary Family, A Vanished Way of Life, and the Unique Child Who Became Theodore Roosevelt* (New York: Simon and Schuster, 1981), 339–40.

Neilson, Helen Parsons, *What the Cow Said to the Calf: Stories and Sketches by Ballie Buck, a Legendary Indian Cowboy* (Gig Harbor, WA: Red Apple Publishing, 1993), 65.

Price, Con. *Trails I Rode* (Pasadena, CA: Trail's End Publishing Co., 1947), 79–81.

Renner, Frederic G. *Charles M. Russell: Paintings, Drawings, and Sculpture in the Amon G. Carter Collection* (Fort Worth, TX: Amon Carter Museum of Western Art, published by the University of Texas Press, Austin, 1966).

Russell, Austin. *C.M.R.: Charles M. Russell, Cowboy Artist* (New York: Twayne Pubishers, 1957), 57.

Russell, Charles M., *Trails Plowed Under, Stories of the Old West* (New York: Doubleday and Company, 1927), 91-100.

"Special Exhibition Paintings and Bronze" (Calgary, AB: *The Stampede*, August 25 to 30, 1919, #22).

Index

Italics indicate artworks by Charles M. Russell
unless otherwise indicated.